MW00811408

Whatever is
LOVELY

Other fantastic books in the growing Faithgirlz™ library

BIBLES

The NIV Faithgirlz Bibles
The NKJV Faithgirlz Bible
NIV Faithgirlz Backpack Bibles

FICTION

Natalie Grant's Glimmer Girls Series

London Art Chase (Book One)
A Dolphin Wish (Book Two)
Miracle in Music City (Book Three)
Light Up New York (Book Four)

Samantha Sanderson Series

At the Movies (Book One)
On the Scene (Book Two)
Off the Record (Book Three)
Without a Trace (Book Four)

Good News Shoes Series

Riley Mae and the Rock Shocker Trek (Book One)
Riley Mae and the Ready Eddy Rapids (Book Two)
Riley Mae and the Sole Fire Safari (Book Three)

The Girls of Harbor View

Girl Power (Book One)
Take Charge (Book Two)
Raising Faith (Book Three)
Secret Admirer (Book Four)

Sophie's World Series (2 books in 1)

Meet Sophie
Sophie Steps Up
Sophie and Friends
Sophie's Friendship Fiasco
Sophie Flakes Out
Sophie's Drama

The Lucy Series

Lucy Doesn't Wear Pink (Book One)

Lucy Out of Bounds (Book Two)

Lucy's "Perfect" Summer (Book Three)

Lucy Finds Her Way (Book Four)

From Sadie's Sketchbook

Shades of Truth (Book One)

Flickering Hope (Book Two)

Waves of Light (Book Three)

Brilliant Hues (Book Four)

NONFICTION

Devotionals

No Boys Allowed

What's a Girl to Do?

Whatever Is Lovely

Shine on, Girl!

That Is So Me

Finding God in Tough Times

Girl Talk

Girlz Rock

Faithgirlz Bible Studies

The Secret Power of Love

The Secret Power of Joy

The Secret Power of Goodness

The Secret Power of Grace

Lifestyle and Fun

Faithgirlz Journal

Faithgirlz Cookbook

True You

Best Party Book Ever!

101 Ways to Have Fun

101 Things Every Girl Should Know

Best Hair Book Ever

Redo Your Room

God's Beautiful Daughter

Everybody Tells Me to Be Myself but I Don't Know Who I Am

faithgirlz™

Allia Zobel Nolan

Whatever is LOVELY

A 90-Day Devotional Journal

ZONDERKIDZ

Whatever is Lovely

This title is also available as a Zondervan ebook. Visit www.zondervan.com/ebooks

Requests for information should be addressed to:
Zondervan, 3900 *Sparks Dr. SE, Grand Rapids, Michigan 49546*

This edition: ISBN 978-0-31075410-7 (hardcover)

Library of Congress Cataloging-in-Publication Data

Zobel Nolan, Allia.
Whatever : livin' the true, noble, and totally excellent life! / by Allia Zobel Nolan.
p. cm.– (Faithgirlz!)
ISBN 978-0-310-72534-3 (softcover)
1. Teenage girls–Prayers and devotions. 2. Christian teenagers–Prayers and devotions.
3. Teenage girls–Religious life. 4. Christian teenagers–Religious life. I. Title.
BV4860.N65 2012
242'.633–dc23 2012015575

Cover design: Micah Kandros Design
Cover illustration: Undrey/Kotoffei/Shutterstock.com
Interior design: Denise Froehlich
Interior illustration: iStockphoto / ©NK08gerd

Printed in the United States of America

---

17 18 19 20 21 /DCI/ 23 22 21 20 19 18 17 16 15 14 13 12 11 10 9 8 7 6 5 4 3

What's Inside

You and Your Thoughts

Whatever's True

Whatever's Noble

Whatever's Right

Whatever's Pure

Whatever's Lovely

Whatever's Admirable

Whatever's Excellent

Whatever's Praiseworthy

Perfect Peace

Dedication

For God and His Holy Spirit,

Whose help and guidance saw me through the writing process; for my patient and supportive husband, Desmond; my friends, Jeanne St. John Taylor and Sara Fudge, PhD; my Zondervan colleagues, Annette Bourland and Kathleen Kerr (who had faith in *Whatever* and helped make it a reality); my editor, Robyn Burwell; my at-home furry office assistant, my cat, Nolan Nolan; and for Faithgirlz everywhere who want "whatever" they think about to be "heavenly."

- *Allia Zobel Nolan*

Section 1

You and Your Thoughts

"You [God] will keep in perfect peace all who trust in you, all whose thoughts are fixed on you!"

Isaiah 26:3 NLT

Devotion 1

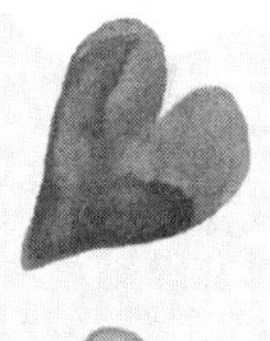

"Finally, brothers and sisters, whatever is true, whatever is noble, whatever is right, whatever is pure, whatever is lovely, whatever is admirable—if anything is excellent or praiseworthy—think about such things."

Philippians 4:8

Whatever . . . More Than Just "Yeah, Right"

Raise your hand if you *don't* use the word "whatever." Thought so.

Everyone uses it, a zillion times a day. Like when your BFF says, "Want to go to the movies?" And you say, "Sure." Then she asks, "What movie?" and you answer, "Whatever." Or while you're downloading music, your little sister says, "Can I paint the cat's nails?" And you answer, "Whatever." It's kind of like saying, "Who cares? Do what you want."

But bet you'd be surprised to know this: Jesus's friend Paul used the "W" word, too, way back when nobody texted and kids wore togas to school. In fact, he repeated it six times in a letter to the Philippians. Why? To emphasize a point—he wanted to teach people that all sin begins first in the mind, with a thought, and that thoughts were linked to actions. So if they thought good things, they'd be more likely to do good things. He also wanted them to realize they could control their thoughts. So he gave them a list to use as a test when they were deciding whether something was worth thinking about. Was the thought "true, noble, right, pure, lovely, admirable, excellent, or praiseworthy?" If not, Paul suggested they fuggetaboutit.

So what's this got to do with you today? Well, what Paul said to the Philippians way back then is just as important now. Our minds are one of the Lord's most awesome gifts. We can use it to glorify him, show him our love, and win ourselves eternal life. Or we can waste it, make the deceiver happy, and wind up where it's decidedly hotter.

The Bible says, "let God transform you into a new person by changing the way you think. Then you will learn to know what God's will is for you ... " (Romans 12:2 NLT).

So start now. Open up your mind and fill it with whatever—whatever is pleasing to God—and see how following the Lord and living the "Whatever Scripture Way," instead of any which way, can make a huge difference in your life.

Food for Thought

Next time a friend says, "Whatever" say, "Philippians 4:8." When she says "Huh?" tell her about the Whatever Scripture way. You might just start a movement.

Second Thoughts

Years before Paul, David also prayed to God for help in avoiding dumb stuff. "Turn my eyes from worthless things," he said, "and give me life through your word" (Psalm 119:37 NLT).

Divine Thoughts

Lord, you've given me such a wonderful gift: my mind. Help me to put it to good use by focusing on you and your Word—especially the Whatever virtues. Amen.

Your Thoughts:

Devotion 2

"May all my thoughts be pleasing to him, for I rejoice in the LORD."

Psalm 104:34 NLT

God-Filtered Thoughts

Researchers tell us we have anywhere from 12,000 to 50,000+ thoughts a day. Whodathunkit?

These thoughts center around friends, parents, schoolwork, money, texts, pets, parties, teachers, food, clothes, that cute boy in assembly, world events, and so much more.

Where does God fit in? We probably think about him during the day when we pray, or if we're reading the Bible, or if we ask for his help. But he's probably not on our minds all the time for basic things, like when we're picking out clothes or choosing a book to read.

Problem is he wants to be. He wants us to filter all our thoughts through him. Because when we do, we'll make better decisions—choices that'll be pleasing to him and better for us. Let's listen in on two girls' trains of thought, and see how that works:

Both Joan and A.J. are at the mall trying on dresses for Linda's party. Joan picks two, and decides the first is boring. She puts on the second, looks in the mirror, and thinks, *Wow, this is, like, way awesome. The other girls will be green. It's a bit tight, but so what? I'm buying it anyway, end of story.* In this scenario, God was totally shut out. Joan never even considered him in her decision.

Now let's see how A.J. handles the same situation. She's torn between two outfits. Her thoughts: *Well, the black outfit would certainly get me noticed. It's a boy-magnet for sure. But would Jesus (or my parents) approve? Ah ... no. I look pretty in the blue dress, and it doesn't look like it was painted on me. So I'll go with that.* A.J. clearly involved God in her considerations. So guess what happened later? Joan's mom took one look at her purchase and said, "Return it." A.J.'s mom loved her choice. So did everyone at the party.

Jesus as a fashion consultant, though? Isn't that a bit much? Nope. The Bible says, "Seek [God's] will in all you do, and he will show you which path to take" (Proverbs 3:6 NLT, emphasis added). So make sure to keep Jesus in the loop—whatever you're thinking.

Food for Thought

God can speak to us through our thoughts. Remember to listen for his voice.

Second Thoughts

Can't make a decision about what to buy? Consider: Is this skirt true to my personality? To the Whatever virtues? Is it lovely, pure, excellent? If not, reconsider.

Divine Thoughts

Lord, help me put you up front, in the engineer's seat, in my thoughts so I can keep on the right track. Amen.

Your Thoughts:

Devotion 3

*"Be careful what you think,
because your thoughts run your life."*
Proverbs 4:23 NCV

U R What You Think

"There's nothing wrong with just thinking," some people say. "You haven't *done* anything. What's the big deal?"

Depends on what you're thinking. Lots of sins begin in your thoughts—sins like pride, envy, covetousness, lust, despair, and dishonesty, which is why God wants you to pay special attention to what's going on in your head.

The Bible says "Temptation comes from our own desires, which entice us and drag us away. These desires give birth to sinful actions. And when sin is allowed to grow, it gives birth to death" (James 1:14–15 NLT).

For example, if you think, *Pam left her bracelet in the locker room again. It would sure look good on me. If you're not careful, your next thought might be, Pam's got a million bracelets. She won't miss this one. Maybe I'll pretend I didn't find it.* And if you keep focusing on this I-want-it, she-won't-miss-it bracelet, you could wind up stealing it.

Yikes! So what's a girl to do?

Try this: When temptation creeps into your head, think "SLAM, LAMB, and SCRAM."

Shut the door (SLAM) on the thought immediately. Don't linger for even a millisecond.

Pray to Jesus, the (LAMB) of God, for grace to resist. Nothing fancy, "Help, Jesus. Quick!" will do.

Remove yourself (SCRAM) ... hop, skip, jump, or run as fast as your Nikes will carry you away from the temptation.

If you're stuck somewhere and can't get away, use God's other power tool: his Word. Try reciting a Bible verse from memory; or list the Ten Commandments, first one to ten, then backwards, ten to one. Think about your favorite Bible hero and what you would say if (that is, when) you meet her.

The Bible says, "Resist the devil, and he will flee from you" (James 4:7 NLT). Jesus did three times in the desert, and the devil disappeared faster than ice on a hot day.

The even better solution, though, is to watch what you think, and keep your thoughts on "Whatever is good" to begin with (Philippians 4:8).

Food for Thought

While people can't look into your mind, God can. What kinds of thoughts is he seeing right now?

Second Thoughts

Make "Beware of the Thoughts," or "U R What U Think," or "Whatever" signs and stick them everywhere to remind you to mind your mind.

Divine Thoughts

Lord, give me your strength to slam the door on temptations and keep my thoughts on you. Amen.

Your Thoughts:

Devotion 4

"Get wisdom; develop good judgment. Don't forget my words or turn away from them."

Proverbs 4:5 NLT

Got Wisdom?

Girl goes to heaven and hands St. Peter a bunch of awards, medals, scholarships, testimonials, diplomas, and degrees.

"I didn't twitter away my time on earth," she says. "I filled my mind with lots of good stuff: biology, geology, zoology. I even learned anthropology."

"And theology?" St. Peter asked. "Did you learn much about God? Did you study his Word? That's the thing that counts up here, I'm afraid."

"Ah, well," the girl stutters, "I didn't. But if you have a Bible handy, it'll just take me a minute. I can speed read."

Okay, maybe that's a bit farfetched. But the point is, God isn't interested in the wisdom we get from worldly books. To him that's all "foolishness" (1 Corinthians 3:19). What he is interested in is in the knowledge we get from his book, a godly wisdom that teaches us to respect and trust the Lord, to live intelligently, and to be honest, just, and fair, making the most of every opportunity for doing good (Proverbs 1:3; Ephesians 5:16).

The Lord gave Solomon this kind of wisdom, and he shares it with us in the 31 chapters of Proverbs. This book not only teaches us ways to act, but also shows us how to make (and keep) friends, the importance of kindness, how to respect our parents, what our responsibility is to the poor, how to handle money, and so much more.

And if we keep these precepts in our heart and let them color the way we think, act, and respond to the Lord, we'll make good decisions and be well on our way to becoming God-focused thinkers. Since many of the Proverbs' affirmations are short, one or two-liners, we could memorize them, or jot our favorites down at the beginning of our school notebooks as reminders of how a wise person responds to this world. Here are a couple (paraphrased) for starters:

- A wise person trusts God.
  Proverbs 3:5

- A wise person is cheerful.
  Proverbs 17:22

Food for Thought

Solomon didn't take his own advice. His downfall? Seven hundred wives and 300 concubines who drained his treasury and worshiped false gods.

Second Thoughts

Solomon says, "Follow the example of the ants and you'll never wind up in the poor house." Read more in Proverbs 6:6-8 NLT.

Divine Thoughts

Heavenly Father, help me to think about things, like the Proverbs, that will make me wise in your eyes. Amen.

Your Thoughts:

Devotion 5

"Run away from the evil desires of youth. Try hard to live right and to have faith, love, and peace, together with those who trust the Lord from pure hearts."

2 Timothy 2:22 NCV

Mind Control

The buzz was that it was awesome. So when a girl at school told Sally she could borrow a popular book everyone was talking about even though her mom had forbidden her to, she took it.

"Now I can't stop thinking about vampires," she told her BFF. "I even dreamed about them last night. I don't know what's wrong with me."

Simple, Sally. The devil's got a hold of your thoughts, and he's having a field day. Like a computer, our minds can pick up a "virus" as well, especially if we don't watch what we put into them. If we "input" bad things, bad things will come out. If we fill our mind with inappropriate stuff, we're going to act inappropriately. If we constantly dwell on what's sinful, we'll ultimately wind up sinning. And the evil one couldn't be happier.

He's just waiting for you to open up that book, or go to that movie, or spend time on that Internet site, so he can infect your thoughts and cause all kinds of havoc. Don't fool yourself into thinking, *Oh, I'm a big girl. I can deal with this stuff.* Because you can't. The things we entertain ourselves with *will* affect us.

Nasty, violent, or impure images and songs will imprint on your thoughts quicker than you can cry "wolf!" And the more we try to stop thinking about them, the deeper they'll dig in. So we can't let them. The Bible says we should "take captive every thought and make it obedient to Christ" (2 Corinthians 10:5 CK). And that's exactly what we have to do. We have to march our thoughts *away* from the devil *into* Jesus's camp, and then barricade the door.

How? We have to take control. We have to limit our minds' access to trash and steer clear of anything—including friends who may pressure us to read inappropriate books or go on improper websites—that can give us the wrong kind of thoughts. We have to train our brains to refrain from "experimenting" with things that will infiltrate our minds and infuse our sinful natures.

Then what? Then, we fill up on the good stuff: God's Word. We read it, think about it, memorize it, and wallpaper our thoughts with it so it fills every corner of our minds.

With God's Word in our hearts and our thoughts on "Whatever" is true, right, noble, pure, lovely, admirable, excellent, and praiseworthy, we'll be less likely to want to read books with imaginary, pointy-tooth characters, or pine over the actors who play these parts in movies (even if they are, like, way cute).

Food for Thought

The Psalmist wrote, "I have hidden your word in my heart, that I might not sin against you" (Psalm 119:11 NLT). Good idea, huh?

Second Thoughts

Not sure about a movie or book? Ask yourself, "Would Jesus read this, even if it was a bestseller? Would he watch this movie?"

Divine Thoughts

Heavenly Father, help me resist worthless entertainment that will fill up my thoughts and take my mind off you. Amen.

Your Thoughts:

Devotion 6

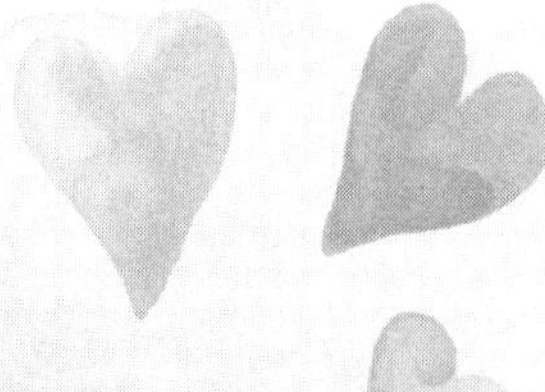

"Can all your worries add a single moment to your life?"

Luke 12:25 NLT

Worry . . . It Boggles the Mind

Worry. It's a thought process that goes on in our heads and has us going in circles. We're anxious about how we look, what people think of us, exams, friendships, parents losing their jobs, global warming, terrorism, acne, sex, the past, the present, the pluperfect.

Still, where would we be without it? I mean, we, like, *have* to worry. That makes everything better.

Don't believe it.

Worry doesn't solve a thing. It as much as tells God we don't trust him; we don't have faith in his plan; and we don't believe he's in charge. We may not mean it, but that's what worry says to the Lord.

"Give all your worries and cares to God, for he cares about you," the Bible tells us (1 Peter 5:7 NLT). Sounds awesome, doesn't it? But, as with a lot of things in our thought-lives, handing over our anxieties, fears, and insecurities to God is easier said than done. Here are some practical anti-worry dos and don'ts that can help:

Do Live for Today. Open up all the wonderful gifts God has put in your life this moment. Don't miss them because your mind is occupied worrying over something that happened yesterday. The Bible says, "This is the day the LORD has made; we will rejoice and be glad in it" (Psalm 118:24 NLT). We cannot change the past, so spending time in it is a waste. However, we can and should enjoy today.

Don't Time Travel. Stay in the present. Don't think about what will happen on Friday, three weeks from now. The Bible says, "Now listen, you who say, 'Today or tomorrow we will go to this or that city ....' Why, you do not even know what will happen tomorrow.... Instead, you ought to say, 'If it is the Lord's will, we will live and do this and that'" (James 4:13-15).

Do Have Faith. Trust God and don't worry, because he wants the best for you. The Bible says, "For I know the plans I have for you ... plans to prosper you and not to harm you, plans to give you hope and a future" (Jeremiah 29:11).

Do Turn to God in Prayer. "Do not be anxious about anything," Paul said, "but in every situation, by prayer and petition, with thanksgiving, present your requests to God" (Philippians 4:6). Jonah did. When the big fish swallowed him, Jonah immediately turned to the Lord in prayer. He said, "In my distress I called to the LORD, and he answered me" (Jonah 2:2). When we're worried, we should turn to God in prayer, too.

Food for Thought

There are approximately 365 Scriptures that tell us not to be afraid, fear, worry, be anxious, or be troubled. See if you can find them all.

Second Thoughts

Keep a worry journal. Jot down what you think will happen, then what actually happened. Be ready to be surprised.

Divine Thoughts

Lord, help me to always remember that whatever happens, you always have my best interests at heart. So I should stop worrying. Amen.

Your Thoughts:

Devotion 7

"A person with an evil heart will find no success,
and a person whose words are evil will get into trouble."

Proverbs 17:20 NCV

Suspicion Free—Yipeeee!

"Hey, thanks for picking up the scarf," Kiley said to Stephanie. "It's, like, so cool. I'll pay you tomorrow."

But after two weeks passed, Stephanie had yet to see her money.

Even worse, Kiley wasn't hanging in the usual places at school. Suspicious Stephanie's thoughts went ballistic: *Kiley's avoiding me. She thinks I'm stupid—that I forgot about the money. Or maybe she thinks I don't need it because my parents are rich.*

Making snap judgments about people—especially when they're negative ones—doesn't say much for us as Christians. God wants us to love our neighbor, and that love "... always trusts, always hopes" (1 Corinthians 13:7). What's more, suspicious thoughts sap the joy from life. They can turn a girl sour—make her think everyone is out to get, gyp, or make fun of her.

The Bible says, "Do not spread false stories against other people" (Leviticus 19:16 NCV). So whether we're imagining wrong things about a person, or saying them out loud, we're not following God's Word. On top of that, we can wind up red-faced and feeling guilty. Suspicions can also end friendships and make others avoid us like yesterday's tuna casserole.

"The Lord knows people's thoughts" (Psalm 94:11 NLT), says the Psalmist. Though we can't look into a person's mind to see what's going on, God can. And here's where trust in him figures in. See, if we believe that our Father wants only the best for us, we can give others the benefit of the doubt, because with God there is no doubt. We can ask him for the grace to stop being suspicious, then start thinking of others the way we'd want them to think of us.

"Trust in the Lord," the Bible tells us, "and do good. Then you will live safely" (Psalm 37:3 NLT).

Eliminating suspicions doesn't mean we have a Mary Poppins' attitude toward everyone. If something's too good to be true, it usually isn't true. The savvy girl uses common sense, thinks things through, and asks God to lead her to the truth. "Fools will believe anything," the Bible says, "but the wise think about what they do" (Proverbs 14:15 NCV).

Oh, and Stephanie? She learned later that Kiley's mom was in an accident. When Kiley returned to school, the first thing she did was give Steph her money.

Food for Thought

Continue doing good even when others let you down. Your good example will shine though, and others may well "glorify God on the day he visits us" (1 Peter 2:12).

Second Thoughts

When something goes wrong, you always give your BFF the benefit of the doubt. You don't jump to conclusions. So why not extend that same courtesy to everyone?

Divine Thoughts

God, I don't want be another Suspicious Stephanie. Help me to think the best of people. Amen

Your Thoughts:

Devotion 8

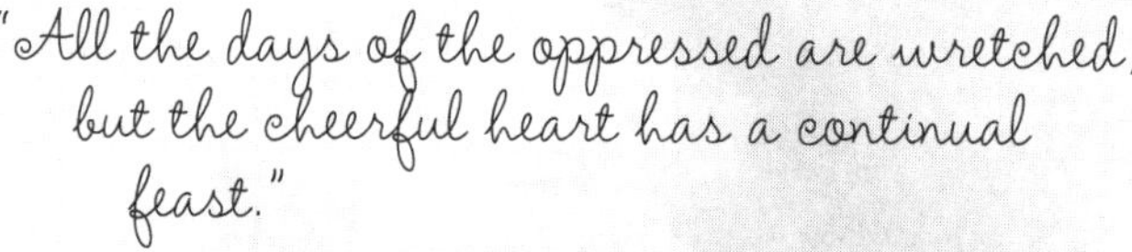

Proverbs 15:15

Change Your Thoughts . . . Change Your Day

My hair looks like I combed it with a rake, you think, and that starts the ball rolling.

This dress is like ROTFLOL ridiculous, and I won't get a new one now that Dad lost his job.

I look like a troll today. Why do I have to be so ugly?

Negative thoughts can hold you captive and multiply like ants at a picnic. But if you take control, put your hope in God and his Word, you can turn things around and have a great day, no matter *what's* going on.

When King David was down in the dumps, he got out of his bad moods by thinking about all the good things God had done for him. When he finished, the Bible says, he was "whistling, laughing, and jumping for joy" (Psalm 9:2 MSG).

"You thrill me, Lord, with all you have done for me!" David wrote. "I sing for joy because of what you have done" (Psalm 92:4 NLT).

David had the right idea. You can't stay in a stinky mood long if you think about how wonderful God is, how many times he has answered your urgent prayers, forgiven you for your mistakes, and gotten you out of really bad scrapes. And like David, remembering instances of God's goodness will surely make you think, *Wow, am I blessed,* instead of, *Boy, I'm depressed.*

What's more, when you feel a bout of the blahs coming on, you can also turn to the Bible for solace and lots of good advice:

Bad hair? The Bible says, "Don't be concerned about the outward beauty of fancy hairstyles.... You should clothe yourselves instead with the beauty that comes from within" (1 Peter 3:3–4 NLT). So fix your hair and forget about it. Then maybe work on your inner self by praying for sick kids who've lost their hair.

No money for new duds? Jesus says, "And why worry about your clothing? Look at the lilies of the field and how they grow. They don't work or make their clothing, yet Solomon in all his glory was not dressed as beautifully as they are" (Matthew 6:28–29 NLT). So maybe you should thank God for the clothes you do have, then use your creativity to combine an outfit in a new and different way.

Not feeling pretty? The Bible says we are "amazingly and miraculously made" (Psalm 139:14 GWT). So if God made you wonderful, maybe you should take his Word and stop thinking you're not. Oh, and here's a tip: a girl can look twice as awesome when she smiles. So why not put on one VBG (Very Big Grin) right now, and go "have a nice day." Okay?

Food for Thought

Like David, we could give ourselves pep talks to chase away the blues. Read Psalm 43:5.

Second Thoughts

The word "joy" appears 259 times in the New Living Bible translation of the Bible, not counting the word "rejoice."

Divine Thoughts

Lord, I can get in a bad mood so easily. Help me to realize just how wonderful my life really is because you're my Savior and you love me. Amen.

Your Thoughts:

Devotion 9

"Make thankfulness your sacrifice to God, and keep the vows you made to the Most High."

Psalm 50:14 NLT

Think "Thanks"

Whatever the circumstances, no matter what, we should always have "Thank You, God" on our minds. After all, the Almighty has given us our life, parents, BFFs, our health, our pets. We can see, hear, speak, smell, taste, and feel. (We could go on forever, but you get the picture.) Let's just say (as the Bible has), "Every good and perfect gift is from above" (James 1:17). Even better, God loved us so much, he gave us the perfect gift: his Son, Jesus.

Now, Jesus continually thanked his Father for everything. That tells us how important an attitude of gratitude must be.

On the hill, in front of a hungry crowd he would feed with a few loaves and fish, "Jesus then took the loaves, gave thanks, and distributed to those who were seated as much as they wanted" (John 6:11).

Before he raised Lazarus from the dead, Jesus looked up

and prayed, "Father, I'm grateful that you have listened to me" (John 11:41 MSG).

Even at the last supper, when his thoughts must have been filled with the terror of what was to come, Jesus gave thanks before he dined with his disciples (Mark 14:22–23).

Okay, but what if we get an "F" on our finals, or don't make the cheerleading team, or our parents divorce? We can't be expected to think *Gee thanks, God* for that.

Oh, but we can, and we should. The Bible says, "give thanks in all circumstances; for this is God's will for you in Christ Jesus" (1 Thessalonians 5:18) and that's a good habit to form for some very good reasons:

It shows God we trust him—not just when things are going our way—but when the bad stuff comes along, too. It proves we believe he's a loving Father who has a plan for us, and though we might not understand what it's all about, *he* does. It shows him we have faith that everything he sends, will, in the long run, be to our benefit.

See, what we're trying to do is to get to the point where we're accepting and grateful to God for everything that comes our way, even when we can't imagine what good can possibly come of a situation.

The Bible says, "And we know that in all things God works for the good of those who love him, who have been called according to his purposes" (Romans 8:28).

We just have one thing to say about that: *Thanks, God.*

Food for Thought

Jesus healed ten lepers. But only one returned to thank him. When God does something spectacular in your life, do you say, "Thank you"?

Second Thoughts

Show family members you appreciate them by creating a hand-made card that says, "For all you do, my thanks to you."

Divine Thoughts

Dear God, remind me not to complain about what I don't have and focus instead on what I do have. Amen.

Your Thoughts:

Devotion 10

"I am the Lord, the one who encourages you.
Why are you afraid of mere humans?
They dry up and die like grass."

Isaiah 51:12 CEV

What Others Think

Hung up about what others think of you? Join the club. We all want to be liked. We all want to be popular. We all want to get that all important "A" of approval.

But how far are *you* willing to go? Would you watch a funny movie with questionable content, just so you could brag about it? Would you join plans to embarrass someone because everyone else is, even though you like the girl? Would you give a friend test answers so she'll tell everyone you're a pal?

It's easy to get sucked in to the approval-seeking trap. A girl named Mary did and came to regret it big-time. To impress a popular girl, Mary hid her beliefs. And though she didn't like the taste of either, she began to smoke and drink with her new friend. She felt guilty at first. But being accepted by the "with-it" clique seemed to make it worthwhile. Or did it? One day, a girl in the group saw Mary leave church with her mom and "accused" her of being a "Jesus freak."

Mary was about to make some lame excuse about church. But she stopped. "When it came right down to it," she admitted, "I just could *not* bring myself to deny Jesus outright. Asking me if I was a Christian woke me up. I didn't care what these people thought any more," she said. "All I could think was, 'Jesus, I'm so sorry.'"

Weeks later, the ring leader Mary wanted to "friend" so badly moved with her family to Detroit.

Mary found out the hard way that people come and people go, taking their approval with them. She also learned that being liked by this one or that one, though it may be tremendously important at the time, might not be so earth-shattering in a week, or a month, or a year.

Truth is, there's only one person whose acceptance really matters: God. And if we're looking for approval, he's the one to go to—because he takes us unconditionally, "as is." And he's for us, even when, like Mary, we mess up and think pleasing others is more important than pleasing him. Our God loves us, warts and all. And to prove it, he gave up his life so that we could live.

Now, would anyone you ever wanted approval from so badly do the same?

Food for Thought

Want to be like Jesus? Forget pleasing people and start pleasing God. "The one who sent me is with me," Jesus said, "for I always do what pleases him" (John 8:29).

Second Thoughts

Paul had the right attitude about approval: "As for myself, I do not care if I am judged by you or by any human court....The Lord is the One who judges me" (1 Corinthians 4:3–4 NCV).

Divine Thoughts

Jesus, help me to realize that when I feel needy, the best place to turn is to that someone who loves me a whole bunch: You. Amen.

Your Thoughts:

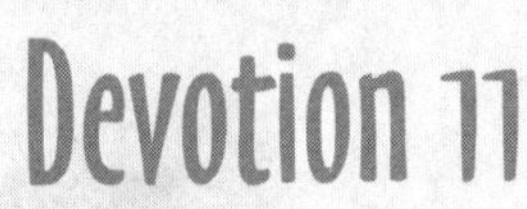

Devotion 11

"People judge by outward appearance, but the Lord looks at the heart."

1 Samuel 16:7 NLT

How NOT to Be a Pharisee

Leslie was a great admirer of Marni. Marni sang in the choir, never missed Bible class, and volunteered at a local shelter. Outwardly, she was a perfect girl of faith. So you can imagine Leslie's shock when she overheard Marni sniggering with her friends.

"You guys wouldn't believe it. Those homeless guys smell like old lockers," she said. "I wouldn't be caught dead there if I didn't need the volunteer points. Next time I go, I'm bringing air freshener."

How a person acts on the outside doesn't always match what's going on inside—in her thoughts or in her heart. The key word here is "acts." Some girls could win Oscars for their performances. They play the part of a good Christian for others to see, while their thoughts and real motives are anything but Christ-like.

Jesus came across quite a few Marnis in his ministry. They were religious leaders of the day called Pharisees. These men were supposed to teach the law of Moses and be examples of how people should live. Instead, they tried to convince themselves and everybody else they were holy because they followed rituals that had nothing to do with worshipping God, but everything to do with putting on a good show.

Jesus saw right through them. And one day, he told them so.

When some Pharisees suggested the disciples were insulting God by not washing their hands before eating, Jesus let them have it. "Hypocrites!" he shouted. "You are so careful to clean the outside of the cup and the dish, but inside you are filthy—full of greed and self-indulgence!" (Matthew 23:25 NLT).

No one likes a phony, especially God. He knows what girls like that are all about. And very often, we do, too. Because no matter how hard they try to hide it, sooner or later girls whose minds are filled with cutting, unkind thoughts will slip and show their true selves. So they're really not fooling anyone.

The Bible says, "get rid of all evil behavior. Be done with all deceit, hypocrisy, jealousy, and all unkind speech" (1 Peter 2:1 NLT).

So let's ask God to keep our hearts sincere, so we can act like Jesus on the outside and think like Jesus on the inside. And let's pray that day by day we can become more Christ-like and genuine—like a faith girl should be—and not wind up wily like a Pharisee.

Food for Thought

The Pharisees tithed on everything, even herbs from their garden. Yet they short-changed everyone when it came to "fairness and compassion and commitment" (Matthew 23:23 MSG).

Second Thoughts

Who may find refuge and shelter with the Lord? "Those who lead blameless lives and do what is right, speaking the truth from sincere hearts" (Psalm 15:2 NLT).

Divine Thoughts

Heavenly Father, help me to be genuine through and through and serve you with the right motives. I pray this in Jesus's name. Amen.

Your Thoughts:

Devotion 12

"A calm and undisturbed mind and heart are the life and health of the body, but envy, jealousy, and wrath are like rottenness of the bones."

Proverbs 14:30 AMP

The Problem with More

Want to live a calmer, less anxious, healthier life? We can. But first we must learn to stop obsessing over what others have, be thankful and content with the blessings God has given us, and quit thinking we can't be happy unless we have a gi-normous helping of "More."

Okay, so the world tells us we need stuff. We have to have stuff. We can't live without stuff. And that includes the latest and greatest of everything from the coolest phones and mobile devices to the hippest designer clothes. Then, of course, our stuff has to be better than anyone else's. And, naturally, we have to have more of it than anyone else. Otherwise, we're losers.

Don't buy into it. Don't be fooled. God has given us more than enough, and that should be our focus. Because if there's one thing that will mess up our heads and eat away at our souls, it's having an unquenchable thirst for stuff that we can't satisfy.

King Solomon got on that merry-go-round, but it didn't make him very merry. Fact is, he was miserable. "No matter how much we see," he said, "we are never satisfied" (Ecclesiastes 1:8 NLT). Though he had the best the world could offer, "There was nothing really worthwhile anywhere," he admitted (Ecclesiastes 2:11 NLT). Bummer.

Then, too, when we're not content with what we already have, our eyes wander. *I have stuff,* we think, *but her stuff is better.* And before we can say "Look at her UGGs," we could wind up breaking a commandment and be guilty of envy. And we *definitely* don't want to go there. Because when envy gets its hooks in us, nothing is as good as it once was. What made us perfectly happy a minute ago won't measure up now.

The Bible says "be satisfied with what you have" (Hebrews 13:5 NLT). Don't envy a person for anything he owns (Deuteronomy 5:21), and "Don't compare yourself with others" (Galatians 6:4 MSG). "If we have bread on the table and shoes on our feet," Paul said, "that's enough" (1 Timothy 6:8 MSG). In other words, God might not give us pots of money and piles of trendy stuff, but he gives us what we need, and then some.

And actually, truthfully, that's plenty. None of us really needs more.

Food for Thought

Some girls who've lost everything in hurricanes and earthquakes have had to learn to make do with very little. Think how you'd feel.

Second Thoughts

Agur, a Proverb writer, had the right idea when he said, "give me neither poverty nor riches! Give me just enough to satisfy my needs" (Proverbs 30:8 NLT).

Divine Thoughts

Heavenly Father, help me to remember when I'm ogling something I don't need, that sometimes less is more. Amen.

Your Thoughts:

Devotion 13

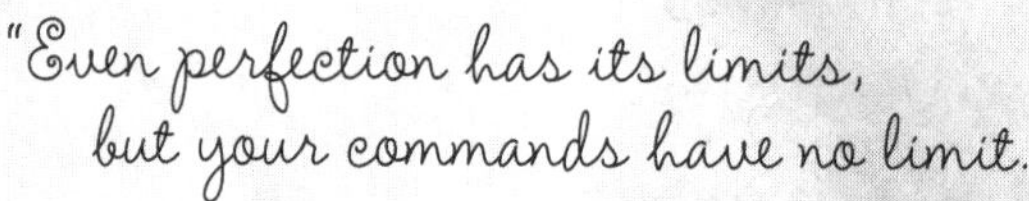

"Even perfection has its limits,
but your commands have no limit.
Oh, how I love your instructions!
I think about them all day long."

Psalm 119:96–97 NLT

Did You Meditate Today?

If someone came up to you and asked, "Do you meditate?" you'd probably tell them, "No, I'm not into that sitting on a rug, chanting OOOOOOMMMMM stuff."

But meditating is more than just getting into a cross-legged position and reciting mantras. The dictionary tells us it's thinking deeply about something, focusing one's complete attention on it, and quietly going over and over that something in your head. (And, no, you can't text, munch candy, or paint your toenails at the same time. Meditating, remember, requires focusing.)

The Psalmists used this thought process to get to know God better. The Bible says, "they delight in the law of the Lord, meditating on it day and night" (Psalm 1:2 NLT). They thought about God's ...

- Unfailing love (Psalm 48:9)
- Mighty acts (Psalm 71:16)
- Decrees (Psalm 119:23)
- Statutes (Psalm 119:99)
- Promises (Psalm 119:148)

You could certainly follow their lead. Okay, so maybe you can't stay up until the wee hours of the morning pouring over the Scriptures like they did. But, for sure, you could take 15-20 quiet minutes or more every day thinking about God and reading his Word.

You could meditate on the story of the Good Samaritan, for example (Luke 10:25-37). You could think about what it means to love your neighbor, who you'd describe as your neighbor, and what you would do if you were in a hurry and saw someone who needed help by the side of the road. Or you could read the Psalms, pick out one that you find particularly beautiful or comforting, and go over how it applies to your life.

Ah, who's got the time for this? You do, if you're serious about loving God and wanting to know him better. What's more, once you experience the peaceful feeling of completely freeing up your mind to think only of God—away from smart phones, ipods, laptops, and TV—you'll find it's something you'll want to do more of. And all this comes with a blessing, too. "But if you look carefully into the perfect law that sets you free," the Bible tells us, "and if you do what it says and don't forget what you heard, then God will bless you for doing it" (James 1:25 NLT).

P.S. Don't be discouraged if other thoughts push their way in. Meditation takes practice. The more you do it, the better you'll become. Start today.

Food for Thought

The Bible says a person who "meditates" upon God's Law is "like a tree planted by streams of water ... whose leaf does not whither—whatever they do prospers" (Psalm 1:3).

Second Thoughts

Take some of your "texting time" and use it to practice thinking about God's Law.

Divine Thoughts

Lord, help me to focus more on activities (like meditating on your Word) that will bring me closer to you. Amen.

Your Thoughts:

Devotion 14

"The heart of the godly thinks carefully
before speaking;
the mouth of the wicked overflows
with evil words."

Proverbs 15:28 NLT

Sorry, Wasn't Thinking

Lauren's big sister, Fran, spent all morning making a cake for the church bake-off. It was her first from scratch, and she was beaming.

"So, what do you think?" Fran asked, "Will it make the top three?"

"Sure," Lauren shot back, "if the judges are blind."

Fran put the cake down and ran out of the kitchen, crying.

"Watch your tongue and keep your mouth shut," the Bible says, "and you will stay out of trouble" (Proverbs 21:23 NLT). Blurting out whatever comes to our minds without thinking can hurt others deeply. Flippant remarks can start arguments and ruin someone's day—and that certainly goes against what Jesus wants us to do: love one another.

Truth is, half of the time, we don't even mean to say the reckless things we do. They just pop into our heads, and because we're *not* thinking, they pop from our mouths, unedited. We let fly with things that seem smart, cool, or funny, but in retrospect are really hurtful and sarcastic.

Jesus warned us about not thinking before we speak. "I tell you that everyone will have to give an account on the day of *judgment* for every empty word they have spoken," he said. "For by your words you will be acquitted, and by your words you will be condemned" (Matthew 12:36–37).

Reason enough to take time to organize your thoughts. Jesus did and calmed an angry mob. When the crowd asked what to do with a woman caught in adultery, Jesus didn't answer immediately. He thought about what his Father would have him say. (Something *we* should do as well.) Then he bent over and wrote something in the dirt. (Was he giving people time to cool off?) When he was ready, he straightened up and said, "Let any one of you who is without sin be the first to throw a stone at her" (John 8:7). That thoughtful answer diffused the situation, and people left without harming the woman.

Remember, there's always *something* gracious, positive, or considerate God will guide us to say, if we let him. No doubt if Lauren hadn't been so quick-lipped, she would have heard the Helper nudging her to show Fran his Spirit of kindness. She could have rejected her barbed comment for something like, "It's a great first try, and I bet the frosting's awesome. Don't forget to save me some."

So let's not let our mouths get ahead of our thoughts. Let's think first, listen for God's voice within us, then answer.

Food for Thought

Proverbs advises, "Even fools are thought wise if they keep silent, and discerning if they hold their tongues" (Proverbs 17:28). Good advice.

Second Thoughts

Use a delaying tactic to gather your thoughts before you speak. Take a deep breath. Sit down, or stand up. Or simply say, "Can I get back to you on that?"

Divine Thoughts

Jesus, remind me to always consider the effect my words will have on others before I start talking. Amen.

Your Thoughts:

Section 2

Whatever's True

Devotion 15

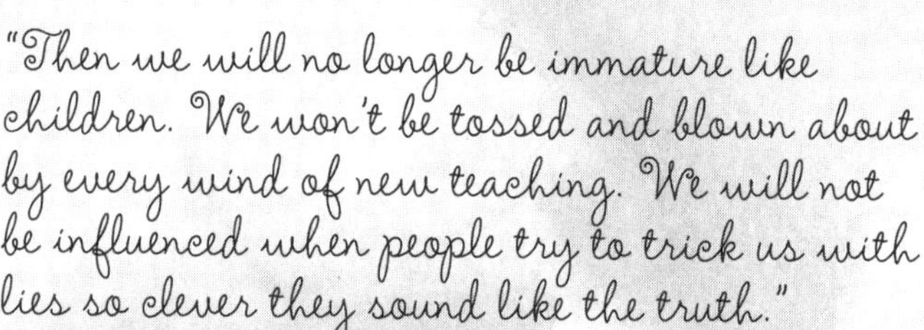

"Then we will no longer be immature like children. We won't be tossed and blown about by every wind of new teaching. We will not be influenced when people try to trick us with lies so clever they sound like the truth."

Ephesians 4:14 NLT

True or False? You Decide

"Wow, that's great!" Hannah said. She was watching a commercial about a cream that promised to clear up acne in three days. Her friend, Martha, rolled her eyes.

"Well, they couldn't have that on TV if it wasn't true," Hannah insisted. "Could they?"

Yup. Yes. You betcha. Fact is we get bombarded with things that aren't real or true a gazillion times a day. Hollywood, Madison Avenue, and the Internet shout, "This is the truth," and "That's the truth," when in reality, what they're pedaling is far from it.

Some people will often talk themselves into believing something is true, and not so much because it is, but because they want it to be. Or because someone else tells them it's okay. Case in point: A girl in Anna's class took her whole report off an Internet site, changed a few words, and handed it to the teacher as her own. And when Anna tried to tell her what she had done was dishonest, the girl said, "I thought about that, but my sister, Jill, said it's okay. It's research." The teacher didn't agree. She gave the girl an F for copying.

The truth can often be twisted or clouded. And sometimes, it's just plain ignored. When God's prophet told the people to repent or they would become exiles, they "were obstinate and stubborn" (Ezekiel 2:4). The Lord told Ezekiel they could know the truth if they wanted to, but they "won't listen, for they are completely rebellious!" (Ezekiel 2:7)

Then too because we act on what we believe is true, we have to find out what *is* true before we act. We have to do our homework. We have to pay attention. We have to go to the source: Jesus.

"I am the way and the truth and the life" (John 14:6). Jesus said. So when doubts arise, or when the world or other kids want you to take something as gospel that doesn't feel right, talk to Jesus. Tell him you need the Helper's guidance. Jesus knows his Holy Spirit will lead you to the Bible. And he knows once you're there, you'll get the answers you need.

So don't take someone else's word about the truth. Take Jesus's word—*the* Word. Once you do, it'll be much easier to separate the truth from falsehoods parading as truth.

Food for Thought

Like Jesus and his Word, the truth is constant. The Bible says God is not like men. Whatever he promises, he does (Numbers 23:19).

Second Thoughts

The Holy Spirit is your true/false barometer; "he will take you by the hand and guide you into all the truth there is" (John 16:13 MSG).

Divine Thoughts

Holy Spirit, thanks for helping me to see the real truth. Amen.

Your Thoughts:

Devotion 16

"If you abide in My word [hold fast to My teachings and live in accordance with them], you are truly My disciples. And you will know the Truth, and the Truth will set you free."

John 8:31–32 AMP

Breaking Free

There's a really powerful tool we can use to fight sin. Like a hammer, it can smash the chains that bind us to wrong doing. Yes, it's God truth, and we can't miss it if we look in the Bible. And once we find it, accept it, and follow it, we don't ever have to be prisoners to sin again.

Take Carrie, for example. Not a day went by that she didn't gossip about Kenisha—the girl who stole her starring role in drama club. Kenisha's voice was lame, Carrie said. She looked like an elephant in the dance number; she brown-nosed Mrs. Finbarr to get the part; and yada, yada, yada. It wasn't long before Carrie's friends became her ex-friends.

So one day, Carrie's remaining BFF took her aside and told her the truth: "Nobody wants to be around you. They're tired of hearing gossip about Kenisha. You have to get a grip, girl," her friend warned. "You have to get in the Word."

Carrie was a believer, so she got the message fast. She was out of control, but wouldn't admit it to herself. Once her friend called her on it, though, she knew she had to do something. And she did. She turned to her Bible for the truth and found it: "For jealousy and selfishness are not God's kind of wisdom. Such things are earthly, unspiritual, and demonic" (James 3:15 NLT). "So get rid of all evil behavior. Be done with all deceit, hypocrisy, jealousy, and all unkind speech" (1 Peter 2:1 NLT).

Carrie wrote the verses in her diary and vowed to follow them. Then she asked God to forgive her and erase the hatred from her heart. She also prayed to Jesus to send the Helper to keep her from returning to her old ways. It was a struggle, for sure. But facing the truth was the step that made change possible.

We can all find ourselves in a similar situation—captives of behaviors we want out of—but can't seem to break free of. Or think we can't. When that happens, remember, the Bible says we don't have to stay slaves to sin. We can break free and become slaves to doing what's right and holy instead (Romans 6:19). The hammer of truth really *can* set us free ... if we let it.

Food for Thought

You can't fix your behavior unless you know it's broken. Read more about knowing what's right and what's wrong in Romans 14:23.

Second Thoughts

Slavery was common in Bible times. That's why Jesus first, and then Paul, used the idea of a slave and his master to explain sin and its hold (Romans 6:19).

Divine Thoughts

Dear Jesus, I don't want sin to keep me a prisoner. Help me to break free and stay free. Amen.

Your Thoughts:

Devotion 17

"Instead, let the Spirit renew your thoughts and attitudes. Put on your new nature, created to be like God—truly righteous and holy."

Ephesians 4:23–24 NLT

Jesus Changes You

Change is the name of the game for tweens. Our bodies, clothes, teachers, friends, pets, boys; our bedtimes; the foods we like—everything's constantly changing.

Then, of course, there's Jesus. He changes us for good. Once we have him in our hearts, we don't look at life the way other girls do. Our priorities are different. When we're "in" with Jesus, we can no longer be "in" with the world.

"So be in both," some girls will say. "Things will be pretty bo-ring if you don't." Ha! They don't know Jesus like we do. He isn't interested in a half-and-half Christian. With him, it's all or nothing. We can't be luke-warm (Revelation 3:16). We have to be full strength. There's no middle of the road.

The Bible says once you become a Christian, you're a new person. You're not the same anymore, "for the old life is gone; a new life has begun!" (2 Corinthians 5:17 NLT).

That's why we don't wear tight jeans and bare midriff fashions. We don't watch films we know we shouldn't, cheat on tests, or obsess over vampire novels, either.

We don't do anything that will jeopardize our relationship with the Savior of the World. That's our goal and it's too important to mess up. Okay, sometimes we don't hit the target, but that's what we're aiming for. And the funny thing is, the closer we get to Jesus, the more we'll notice the change. Instead of feeling we're missing out, we'll begin to feel far better off—because in comparison with the love of Jesus, this worldly stuff can look pretty lame.

That's what happened to Paul.

"Yes," he said, "all the things I once thought were so important are gone from my life. Compared to the high privilege of knowing Christ Jesus as my Master, firsthand, everything I once thought I had going for me is insignificant.... I've dumped it all in the trash so that I could embrace Christ" (Philippians 3:8–9 MSG).

Knowing Jesus changed Paul big-time. It changes us, too, and will continue to do so if we stay close to him.

Meantime, let's show everyone we have our priorities straight. We're not embarrassed to think about heavenly things. And we'd much rather focus on the sublime instead of the stupid.

Food for Thought

Three guesses who never changes? You got it. "I am the Lord," the Bible says, "and I do not change" (Malachi 3:6 NLT).

Second Thoughts

Change is good. So is routine. Daniel prayed three times a day, religiously (Daniel 3:10). Sounds like a good habit to form.

Divine Thoughts

Jesus, send your Spirit to keep me focused on the good things in life ... anything that has to do with you. Amen.

Your Thoughts:

Devotion 18

"Instead, you must worship Christ as Lord of your life.... Keep your conscience clear. Then if people speak against you, they will be ashamed when they see what a good life you live because you belong to Christ."

1 Peter 3:15–16 NLT

Truth Triumphs

"Did you tell her she had *some* nerve? I would have," Felicity's BFF said when she heard Agnes accused Felicity of stealing money.

"I thought about it," Felicity answered. "But I took a deep breathe and just said: 'Look, I gave the card to Miss Evans. I don't know what happened after that. And that's the truth.'"

A week later, Felicity was on the receiving end of one sheepish apology. Agnes found the money she was missing in the secret compartment of her backpack. And when she called Felicity to explain, she couldn't stop saying she was sorry.

"So did you, like, totally ream her out?" Felicity's BFF asked.

"Nah. I just said: 'I knew the truth. And God knew the truth; and now YOU know the truth. I didn't take any money.'"

It's a real downer when girls accuse us of something we didn't do. We're incensed, humiliated, and helpless. When this happens, we can get angry and tell the accusers off, then run around like a crazed chicken trying to clear our names. Or, we can do what Jesus did: "He did not return abuse ... he did not threaten; but he trusted himself to the one who judges justly" (1 Peter 2:23 NRSV).

Handing over false accusations to God and waiting to be vindicated is the smart way to go (though perhaps not always the easiest). On the other hand, relying exclusively on ourselves—especially when we're ticked off at an obvious injustice—might be a recipe for trouble. The Bible says, "And don't sin by letting anger control you" (Ephesians 4:26 NLT). In this case, that's a real possibility. And wouldn't it be, like, a total drag if we wound up doing something wrong while we were trying to prove we didn't do something wrong?

Besides, relying on God—the best thing to do in every circumstance anyway—comes with a guarantee. The Bible says if we trust the Lord, he'll help us. We just have to hold on to the truth, be patient, and wait for him to act (Psalm 37:5–7). Oh, and FYI, the good news is when God vindicates, He *really* vindicates.

"[God] will make your innocence radiate like the dawn," the Bible tells us "and the justice of your cause will shine like the noonday sun" (Psalm 37:6 NLT).

Ah ... that ought to shake up our accusers. You think?

Food for Thought

David, Moses, Joseph, Job, Paul, and Jesus were all falsely accused. But they never let go of the truth, and God delivered them.

Second Thoughts

There are seven things God really detests. One is "a false witness who pours out lies" (Proverbs 6:19 NLT).

Divine Thoughts

Dearest Jesus, calm me when I get accused of something I didn't do, so I can think clearly and not let anger make me sin. Amen.

Your Thoughts:

Devotion 19

"God hates cheating in the marketplace."
Proverbs 11:1 MSG

Cheating: It's a Big Deal

It took Gina a gazillion hours of research, writing, and rewriting, but she finally finished her science project. Not surprisingly, she was thrilled with herself. But God was even more delighted. Why? Because Gina met her challenge using a technique he totally approves of: She did the work herself—without cheating.

Cheating goes on all the time at schools, whether it's paying for papers from Essays R Us, copying work that isn't ours, or lending work to others. Those who've succumbed rationalize it with excuses about too much homework, the drive to get good grades, peer pressure, yada, yada, yada. Girls talk themselves into believing they're being unfairly overburdened with work, so they feel justified in making their own rules. Expert cheaters will also tempt others by appealing to their loyalty. A *real* BFF, they'll say, would let them copy homework, or give them answers to tests.

Why the matter-of-fact attitude about cheating? Because some girls rationalize that cheating is no big deal. These same girls would never dream of stealing something from a store. But they'd think nothing of snatching something off the Internet.

Fact is, though, taking something that doesn't belong to you is stealing, (and it's lying too because you're saying something is yours when it isn't). So girls who cheat commit not one, but two sins. And these sins come with consequences.

The Bible says, "Your iniquities have separated you from your God; your sins have hidden his face from you, so that he will not hear" (Isaiah 59:2). The sin of cheating puts a wedge between us and God. And that, for sure, is a very big deal.

Girls may brag about getting away with cheating. But the Bible sums it up in Proverbs: "Stolen bread tastes sweet, but it turns to gravel in the mouth" (Proverbs 20:17 NLT). Bah!

Cheating has other consequences, too, such as—

- Losing the special feeling that accomplishment brings—the "Yay Me, I Did It!" feeling.
- Never knowing if we really could have done the work.
- Failed grades, suspension, and being shunned.
- Becoming addicted to cheating. (Cheat once, we'll want to do it again.)

The Bible says, "The Lord approves of those who are good, but he condemns those who plan wickedness" (Proverbs 12:2 NLT). So let's please the Lord and don't even think about cheating.

Food for Thought

Cheating would never pass the Whatever test. It's not true, noble, right, pure, lovely, admirable, excellent ... and for sure not praiseworthy.

Second Thoughts

Overwhelmed with schoolwork? Pray for a double dose of God's amazing grace. Then talk to your parents, teachers, and older siblings about ways you can get help.

Divine Thoughts

Heavenly Father, help me see cheating for what it really is: stealing and lying. Then please stand by and help me resist. (It's hard.) Amen.

Your Thoughts:

Devotion 20

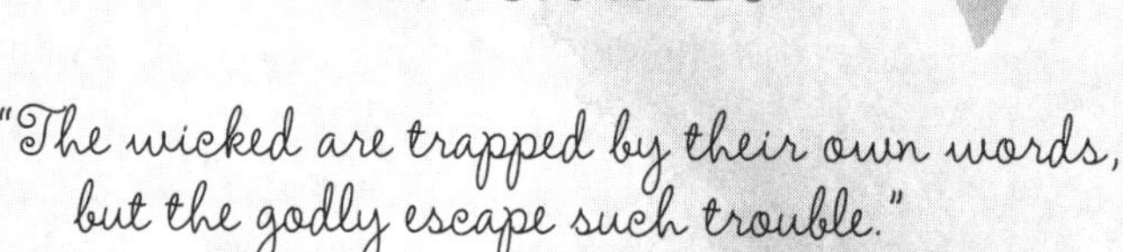
"The wicked are trapped by their own words,
but the godly escape such trouble."
Proverbs 12:13 NLT

A Lie Is a Lie Is a Lie

If you took a poll of ninety gazillion girls, it would probably be hard to find one who never told a white lie. And they would all have similar reactions:

"Oh, come on," they'd say. "Everyone tells white lies sometimes. You know, like, so they don't hurt people's feelings."

Girls tell little white lies for other reasons, too: they're looking to make a good impression, don't want to look stupid, don't want to appear rude or unfriendly, or they're afraid people won't like them. The list goes on and on. Most get snagged, though, because they want to please people—especially their BFFs. They just can't stand to say that itty, bitty, two-letter word, "No." So they lie, and say "Yes" instead. This almost always backfires. Here's an example.

Sheila and her new BFF, Alice, were on the beach, giggling and talking about the school trip. Sheila was starting to feel the heat, though. She had never really been into sunbathing because her skin was fair, and she always got burnt. Alice felt the same way, actually, but since they had just become BFFs, neither girl knew this about the other.

"Want to go, now, Alice?" Sheila asked, when she thought she'd have sunstroke.

"I'm okay," Alice answered, even though she was roasting.

A half-hour passed, and when she couldn't take the rays another minute, Sheila said, "Alice, I've, like, got to get out of here. I'm, like, so red, I'm turning blue."

"But I thought YOU wanted to stay," Alice said. "I was ready an hour ago."

"Oh, no, Alice," Sheila groaned. "I said 'Yes' because it's what I thought *you* wanted." After that, the two girls made a pact to always tell each other the truth ... no matter what. No more "little white lies."

Whether it's telling your BFF she looks good when she doesn't, or telling friends "Yes" when you mean "No," white lies are a problem because we're not being honest. And nine times out of ten, the real truth surfaces, and we wind up hurting/offending people anyway. Then, too, girls lose faith in us. They can't depend on us. They don't trust what we say anymore.

Even more serious, though, is that by making our friends feel good, we've made God feel badly.

Jesus hit the nail on the head when he said, "All you need to say is simply 'Yes' or 'No'; anything beyond this comes from the evil one" (Matthew 5:37). It's advice that could save you from really getting burnt.

Food for Thought

If your BFF is the kind of friend you want her to be, she wouldn't want you to lie to make her feel good anyway.

Second Thoughts

Word expert Michael Quinion says the term "white lie" was first used in the 18th century to mark the difference between an evil lie and a lie with no bad intentions. Still, a lie is a lie.

Divine Thoughts

Dearest Jesus, I have to realize no matter what I call them, white, black, or orange, lies are still lies. So I need to stop telling them. Help me, Lord. Amen.

Your Thoughts:

Devotion 21

"So we know that God loves us. We depend on it. God is love. Anyone who leads a life of love shows that he is joined to God. And God is joined to him."

1 John 4:16 NIrV

Your Father Loves You

There's one truth we never have to wonder about it: God loves us. Eureka! No matter how many times we think of that, it has to be mind-boggling. God, the Almighty, Powerful Creator of this whole entire universe ... loves us.

And when God says he loves us, we know it's not just idle words. There's power behind it. And to prove it, he left his home, took on human form as Jesus, and came to earth to pay the price for our sins. He died so we could live. Now, *that's* love! "This is how we know what love is," the Bible tells us, "Jesus Christ laid down his life for us" (1 John 3:16).

Though our hearts know all this, it's still hard to get our minds around it. The Bible tells us God's love "is too great to understand fully" (Ephesians 3:19 NLT). But Jesus told us to try thinking of it this way: The love he has for us is like the love his Father has for him, a relationship so strong, nothing can come between them. Jesus wants us to have that kind of relationship with the Father, too.

How? Jesus gave us the heads up on that as well. "When you obey my commandments, you remain in my love, just as I obey my Father's commandments and remain in his love" (John 15:10 NLT).

Does that mean if we mess up, God's love changes? Nope. God never changes, and neither does his love. But our perception of it might. When we sin, we feel guilty. We're embarrassed and we think, *How could God possibly love me after this?* And those feelings put up a wall between us and God. But God's love is still there. (It's like when we disobey our parents, they don't love us any less. They're just disappointed in us.)

When we obey God, though, there's no sin barrier. So we can draw even closer and experience the full intensity of God's love. And, boy, is that awesome!

Fact is there's nothing that can separate us from his love. Death can't, and life can't. The angels can't, nor the demons can't. Whether we are high above the sky, or in the deepest ocean, nothing in all creation will ever be able to separate us (Romans 8:38–39). God will never let us go. And he'll never stop loving us. And that's the truth. SFETE (Smiling From Ear to Ear).

Food for Thought

When things don't make sense, remember, everything that happens comes wrapped in God's love.

Second Thoughts

On an index card, write a list of ten loving things that God has done for you. On the back, list ten ways you can show God you love him. Refer to it often.

Divine Thoughts

Jesus, I can rely on one thing to be true: you love me. Even better, you know all about me, and you still love me. Awesome! Amen.

Your Thoughts:

Devotion 22

"So the Word became human and made his home among us. He was full of unfailing love and faithfulness. And we have seen his glory, the glory of the Father's one and only Son."

John 1:14 NLT

Jesus Is God

People are always trying to figure Jesus out. Who is he, really?

Christians believe Jesus is God, and we consider the Bible his certificate of authenticity. In it, we find countless stories of miracles no ordinary man could have performed, and claims a person would have to be either bonkers ... or God ... to make. Statements such as, "The Father has sent me," and "This is what my Father wants," and "Anyone who has seen me has seen the Father" (John 20:21; John 6:40 MSG; John 14:9). Jesus also admitted the truth when the Pharisees asked him point blank if he was God's Son. "Yes I am," he answered (Luke 22:70 TLB).

Okay, for sure, God coming down from heaven and taking a human form is a gi-normous concept.

Even Jesus's BFFs had problems with that. Their eyes saw Jesus the man. But for some reason, their minds couldn't get a grip on the God part of him—which probably explains their getting excited over things Jesus could easily handle—like feeding a crowd of 5,000 or calming a storm.

Of course, the Pharisees were always bugging Jesus for a sign, as though Jesus would do a miracle "on demand," like pay-per-view TV.

That wasn't Jesus's style. He taught, healed, and preached. He told people everything they needed to know and do to be saved. Then he left it up to them.

The Bible says, "He came to his own people, and even they rejected him" (John 1:11 NLT). And even fewer believed he was God.

Peter did. He said others may believe Jesus was a dead prophet come to life. But he believed Jesus is "the Son of the living God" (Matthew 16:15-16).

Martha, a close friend, did, too. "Yes, Lord," she told Jesus. "I believe that you are the Messiah, the Son of God" (John 11:27).

Thomas, the apostle, believed, but only after putting his hands into Jesus's wounds. Then he cried out, "My Lord and my God!" (John 20:28).

Until Jesus comes again, there will always be girls who'll want proof.

"If you're really God, Jesus, let my dog live," they'll say. Or, "If you're really God, don't let my parents divorce." Others will say Jesus was just "a very good man," or a "great teacher."

As Christians, though, we believe the real truth: Jesus was "a very good man" and a "great teacher." But, more importantly, he is the one the world was waiting for: the only Son of God.

Food for Thought

Jesus preached until he was blue in the face, cured people, suffered, died, and rose again ... and people *still* wanted a sign!!!

Second Thoughts

Who knew Jesus was the Son of God right off the bat? Demons in two possessed men. They called Jesus "the Son of God" (Luke 4:41).

Divine Thoughts

Dearest Jesus, I love you, believe in you, and pray that like Thomas did, the whole world will proclaim you as their "Lord" and their "God." Amen.

Your Thoughts:

Devotion 23

"[Satan] was a murderer from the beginning, not holding to the truth, for there is no truth in him. When he lies, he speaks his native language, for he is a liar and the father of lies."

John 8:44

Liar, Liar, Pants on Fire

If there were a prize for lying, the devil would win it. Telling whoppers is what he does best. Like, "It's okay to sneak five dollars out of your mom's purse. You're just borrowing it." Or, "Swearing is no big deal; everybody does it."

The devil also uses half-truths to confuse us, like, "Okay, yes, this website has sex on it. But this is educational. It has important information you need."

Yeah, right.

We don't call Satan the "deceiver" for nothing. Besides out-and-out lies, he plants doubt in our minds so we question God, ourselves, our purpose. And he loves playing up to our ego with thoughts like, *You have a RIGHT to this and that,* or *You're not going to let them do THAT to you?*

Poor Eve got sucked in. "You won't die," Satan fibbed to her about the apple (Genesis 3:4 NLT). So she bit, and with one crunch, the devil got what he wanted: sin was in. Eve was out. What's more, because of sin, misery entered the world, too. And who better to blame that on? God, of course.

See, the devil's a lot more than a Halloween character. He's a vicious enemy who uses lies to cause pain, lead us into sin, and tempt us away from Jesus. We can't fight him alone. But we don't have to. We have God and his "mighty power" (Ephesians 6:10). And that power is far greater than the devil, so we don't have to be afraid.What's more, we have the Holy Spirit's protective armor to rely on (Ephesians 6:11-17). Here's how it works:

- ***The Helmet of Salvation:*** protects our mind by reminding us we are saved and claimed by Jesus through his death.
- ***The Breastplate of Righteousness:*** helps us remember Satan can't hurt us if we do what's right.
- ***The Belt of Truth:*** points out the devil's lies by upholding Jesus's truth.
- ***The Sandals of Peace:*** provide support so we have a strong foothold.
- ***The Shield of Faith:*** wards off the devil's "flaming arrows."
- ***The Sword of the Spirit and the Word of God:*** cut straight through the devil's lying defense.

BTW, for maximum protection against Satan, it's suggested we put on God's armor every day. It's light. It won't rust. And it has a lot more staying power than Tommy Hilfiger. And that's the truth.

Food for Thought

The deceiver was no match for Jesus, who drove him and his lies away by quoting Scripture. Read about it in Matthew 4:1-10.

Second Thoughts

"When Satan comes knocking at my door," a friend's mom told her son, "I say to Jesus, 'Will you please get that?'" Good one, huh?

Divine Thoughts

Jesus, please help me recognize the devil's lying whispers and trust in your faithful power and promises to defeat his schemes. Amen.

Your Thoughts:

Section 3

Whatever's Noble

Devotion 24

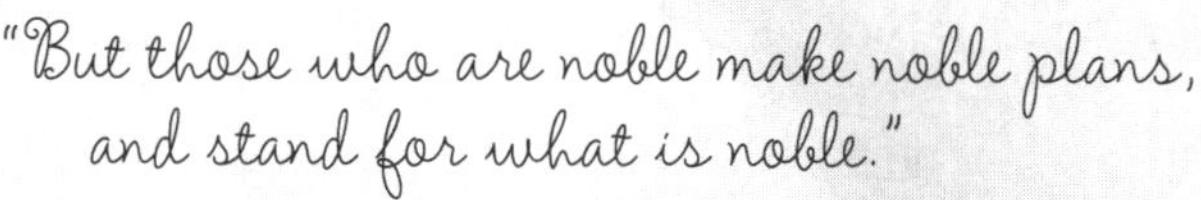

Isaiah 32:8 MSG

Living the Whatever Life

Whatever girls are adopted daughters of the King, and that makes us royalty. Because everyone knows who our Father is, we're held to a higher standard than other girls. So, we not only should *think* about whatever's true, noble, right, pure, lovely, admirable, excellent, or praiseworthy, we should also *tailor our behavior* to those values as well.

Yikes! That means all eyes are on us. We have an important job to do. We have to show others what our Father is like by becoming more like our Lord, Jesus. The Bible says it's as though, "God were making his appeal through us" (2 Corinthians 5:20). We've been chosen by God to be his "instruments to do his work and speak out for him, to tell others of the night-and-day difference he made for you" (1 Peter 2:9 MSG). It also says we "must be an example to them by doing good works of every kind" (Titus 2:7 NLT).

Okay, then, so what should we do?

- We demonstrate our faith by our lives.
- We serve, rather than being served.
- We trust God to lead us, rather than be led by the world.
- We're peacemakers, rather than troublemakers.
- We spread the Word, rather than dish the dirt.
- We share, rather than keep everything for ourselves.
- We forgive.
- We don't try to get even when someone embarrasses us.

As representatives of our Father, Whatever girls are also expected to obey the will of the King, conduct ourselves in a manner befitting our noble rank, act for the good of others by sticking up for what's right, and treat others the way we want to be treated. This means—

- We're loyal to our faith and our Father.
- We stand by friends when others pick on them.
- We lose gracefully.
- We act nicely to girls who hate us and help them out when they need it.
- We sit with girls everyone else ignores on the bus.

- We take the part of another who is wrongly accused.
- We speak out to a teacher, big brother, or an adult when someone is getting badly bullied.

Tall order, we know. But the Bible tells us, "From everyone who has been given much, much will be demanded" (Luke 12:48). And for sure, Whatever girls have been blessed with oodles.

"Once you were not a people," the Bible tells us, "but now you are the people of God" (1 Peter 2:10). We're daughters of the King.

Food for Thought

Want to follow the good example of a super-noble woman? Try Mary, mother of Jesus. She has all the Whatever qualities and more.

Second Thoughts

The Bible tells us, "A wife of noble character.... is worth far more than rubies." Read more in Proverbs 31:10-31.

Divine Thoughts

Dearest Father, sometimes I act like a princess, but not the noble kind. Help me to be humble and thankful, instead of demanding and pouty. Amen.

Your Thoughts:

Devotion 25

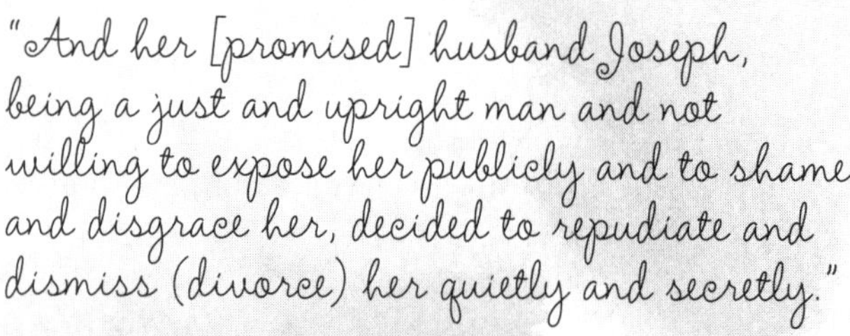

The Honorable Thing

Mary's husband, Joseph, was truly a noble kind of guy—not just because of who he was (Matthew says Joseph came from the royal line of King David, [Matthew 1:1-16]), but because of the honorable way he handled the confusing events surrounding Jesus's birth: with a merciful heart, a willingness to accept responsibility, and a humongous faith in God.

We could learn lots from him.

Okay, so we all know the story. Mary, who was to be Joseph's wife, appeared to have been unfaithful, a slap in the face to Joseph. (And back then, the penalty for such behavior was for the town to stone the accused to death.)

But even more agonizing was the heartache. To Joseph, Mary was the poster girl for everything pure and wholesome. And to have this ideal shattered was difficult for him to take.

Still, being a just man, his conscience wouldn't let him

look the other way. But being a caring man, his heart made him refuse to publicly shame her. What to do?

Someone with less self-control might have looked at Mary and gone ballistic. But Joseph kept his emotions in check. He didn't act rashly.

Someone more self-centered may have thought, *I'm humiliated. How could she do this to ME?* But Joseph didn't focus on his own pain. He focused on Mary's.

Lesson #1: Even when things look bad, don't make snap judgments. Don't react in anger.

Someone not as forgiving may have thought, *She's a disgrace! I'll teach her to betray me!* But Joseph wasn't into revenge. He decided to break things off quietly.

Lesson #2: If you think someone has wronged you, showing compassion (while it's super hard) is the noble thing to do.

Mary's Joseph was not only an honorable man, but also a man of immense faith. Though he must have been totally confused, he trusted God. And when the Lord revealed the truth in a dream, that God wanted him to marry Mary, and that she was having God's Son, he didn't smack his head and say, "This is too much!"

Lesson #3: Mercy triumphs; revenge isn't noble, dignified, or godly.

Like Mary, Joseph willingly and humbly accepted the role God had given him as protector of his Son.

And just think: If Joseph hadn't done the honorable thing, there would have been no happy ending for the rest of us.

Food for Thought

All good friendships and close relationships are built on trust. Joseph trusted Mary and they both trusted God. What would you have done?

Second Thoughts

What do you do when you don't know why things are happening the way they are? Read 2 Corinthians 4:8 for the answer.

Divine Thoughts

Dearest God, help me to do the honorable thing, like Joseph, when I'm faced with a sticky situation. Help me to do what honors you. Amen.

Your Thoughts:

Devotion 26

"And work with a smile on your face, always keeping in mind that no matter who happens to be giving the orders, you're really serving God."

Ephesians 6:7 MSG

The Noblest Profession: Babysitter?

Any job we do can be holy and noble if we do it for God's glory. Even babysitting? Yup. Even jobs like "potato peeler" or "messy room cleaner-upper?" You betcha. In fact, all work is noble because it's part of God's plan. And if we do it cheerfully and to the best of our ability, "you will receive an inheritance from the Lord as a reward" (Colossians 3:24). Wow!

See, when God made Adam and Eve and put them in Eden, he didn't just leave them there to catch rays and drink lemonade. He saw they needed something to do. So he gave them the first jobs—tending the Garden (Genesis 2:15) and naming the animals (Genesis 2:20). It was only after the Fall that work became harder and not so fun.

Still, we all have to work. It's not an option. But we do have a choice in how we go about it. The Bible says, "whatever you do, do it all for the glory of God" (1 Corinthians

10:31 NLT). With this attitude, we can change even monotonous projects into "get-close-to-God" opportunities. And if we get a reputation as a good worker, God won't be the only person to notice.

Becky's clients, some of them non-believers, have high praise for her. She takes an interest in the kids she babysits. Sometimes she'll read to them, or play games, or work on creating crafts. She glorifies God by witnessing through her good example and being the best caretaker ever. Her payoff? She pleases God and gets repeat customers.

Izzy, on the other hand, shows up late and acts like she's doing clients a favor. She seems more interested in what videos they have than in the kids' bedtime. She plops the children in front of the TV, then sticks her earbuds in and goes to text-ville. Her efforts aren't pleasing to God, and her clients have stopped calling.

"Don't just do what you have to do to get by," the Bible says, "but work heartily, as Christ's servants doing what God wants you to do" (Ephesians 6:6 MSG). That will certainly please the "Boss." And that's the cool part. It's not the title of the job or the kind of work we do that gives it value or makes it pleasing to God. It's the love and the effort we put into it.

Food for Thought

"Bloom where you are planted," is an old saying. Paul learned how and you can, too. Read his secret in Philippians 4:11-13.

Second Thoughts

Some girls think they're "entitled" to everything. That wouldn't have gone over with Paul, who said if a person doesn't work, he doesn't eat (2 Thessalonians 3:10).

Divine Thoughts

Dearest God, help me to remember whatever work I do is really for you. Amen.

Your Thoughts:

Devotion 27

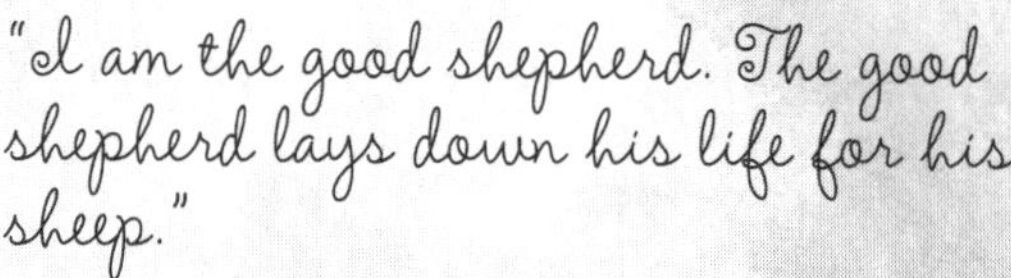

John 10:11

How Do You Spell Noble? J.E.S.U.S.

Who's the noblest person who ever lived?

A king? A shepherd? A businessman?

Guess shepherd? You got it. Jesus, the Good Shepherd, loved us so much he did the noblest thing anyone in the whole universe ever did: He stood in for us and took the punishment we deserve. He suffered pain we can't even imagine so we don't have to. He washed away our sins with his blood. And he did it freely—no one forced him (John 10:18).

But when Jesus tried to explain this—the fact that he was the Good Shepherd who would ultimately die for his sheep—the crowds didn't "get" it. Since back then, lots of people tended sheep for a living, for sure, this should have been the perfect example. Yet they still didn't understand. Why? Because they didn't want to—they stubbornly refused. They would not accept

Jesus (John 10:26) as the Son of God, their Good Shepherd, their Savior. We do, which is why we can relate.

We understand the message Jesus tried to convey: that a really good shepherd cares for his sheep like cherished children and that he makes sure they are well-fed. He nurses them when they're sick or injured. When they're frightened, he calms them. A good shepherd protects his sheep from predators and thieves. He finds them shelter and guards them through the night. And if a lamb wanders off, the good shepherd will go, find it, and bring it home (Luke 15:3–5).

We believe Jesus does all that and more. He feeds us, heals us, comforts us. He defends us against our enemies, watches over us, gives us rest, and even though he has a gazillion sheep, he'll always search for the one that got away.

We also believe that because Jesus was the noblest of shepherds, willing to lay down his life for his sheep, he triumphed over death, rose to live again, and won the right for us to be with him forever. "I give them eternal life," he told the Jewish leaders. "No one can snatch them away from me" (John 10:28 NLT).

Of course, there's nothing we could ever give Jesus to repay him. But, if we think about it, there are things a sheep would automatically do for a caring shepherd that we could do for ours: listen for his voice, follow him closely, and trust him completely.

Food for Thought

Next time you feel like a lost sheep—scared and alone—read John 10, Luke 15:1-7 and Psalms 23 to see how much you're loved.

Second Thoughts

Jesus was the Good Shepherd to the end. Even on the cross he brought a sinner (the criminal next to him) home.

Divine Thoughts

Sweet Jesus, you are truly my good and noble shepherd. Help me to go where you lead me and love you like you love me. Amen.

Your Thoughts:

Devotion 28

"Never let loyalty and kindness leave you!
Tie them around your neck as a reminder.
Write them deep within your heart."
Proverbs 3:3 NLT

Through Thick and Thin, Sneezes and Buggers

"How U stnd it?" Molly texted Bernadette. "Beth sneezes 100 xs a day. (Watch 4 flying buggers!) Dump her & hang w/us. We B alrgy-free."

"Thnx. No can do," Bernadette replied. "Beth is BFF, buggers & all."

Goodie for Bernadette. She gets the Noble Friend of the Year Award. She knows what faithfulness means. And though it may be annoying, she won't dump a friend because of a few sniffles. She's living what the Word says: "A friend is always loyal" (Proverbs 17:17 NLT).

Ruth, the Moabite, believed in loyalty, too. And, boy, did God bless her. After her husband and all the men in his family died, her mother-in-law, Naomi, told Ruth and her sister-in-law to go back to their families. But Ruth loved and respected Naomi. So even though it meant giving up everything, Ruth stuck by her. "Don't force me to leave you; don't make me go home," she said. "Where you go, I go; and where you live, I'll live" (Ruth 1:16 MSG).

Some commitment! And because of it, God changed the whole course of Ruth's life. She not only got to stay with Naomi, marry a wealthy relative, and become great-grandma to King David, but she also wound up becoming an ancestor to Jesus. Awesome!

Okay, but for sure, any mention of loyalty has to come back around to Jesus. As with most noble values, he's the best example of faithfulness we have. Though people called him crazy, a fake, and a blasphemer—he'd never deny his Father. Even when his BFFs begged him to come cure their brother, Lazarus, he didn't side with them. Instead, he stayed loyal to his Father's will and waited until the timing was right.

That's what our Father wants from us, too: our fierce commitment, and no divided loyalties. God "is a God who is jealous about his relationship with you," the Bible says (Exodus 34:14 NLT). That means he wants girls who'll be more devoted to him and his Word than to TV shows, music, or their BFFs; girls who'll stick by him around believers and non-believers; girls who'll un-attach themselves from material things so they can attach themselves to him.

Actually, what he expects is for us to be as loyal to him as Ruth was to Naomi. In others words, he wants us to leave behind our false gods and the things we make into idols, and follow him.

Food for Thought

God's loyalty is gi-normous. The Bible tells us he'll never fail or forsake us; nothing can come between us. He'll always forgive us. Read about it in Hebrews 13:5; Romans 8:38; 1 John 1:9.

Second Thoughts

The Bible says, "Love never gives up, never loses faith, is always hopeful, and endures through every circumstance" (1 Corinthians 13:7 NLT). Jesus's faithfulness cost him his life.

Divine Thoughts

Heavenly Father, please help me to be faithful to you always. Amen.

Your Thoughts:

Devotion 29

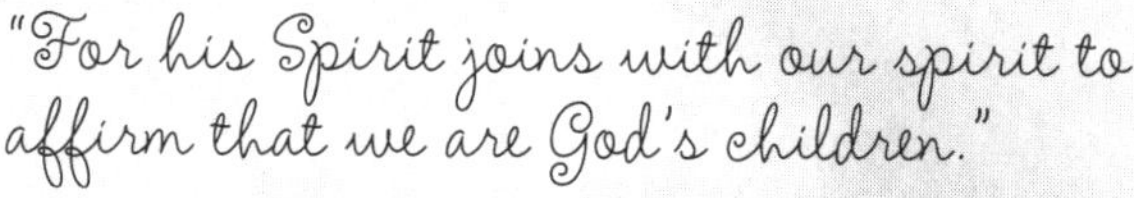
"For his Spirit joins with our spirit to affirm that we are God's children."

Romans 8:16 NLT

The Daughter of the King

When we accept Jesus, something wonderful happens. We go from ordinary girl to adopted child of God—from everyday commoner to royal princess and co-heir to the throne.

How cool is that? Still, our role as princess will be way different than the ones we see in the movies—you know, where the girl prances around the palace wearing a flowing gown and a tiara, giving orders.

As daughters of *our* Heavenly Father, the King, instead of demanding everything our hearts desire, we'll have to give up stuff—riches and flashy trappings of this world—so we can inherit the treasures of the next.

We'll also have to forfeit behaviors that are inappropriate for the daughters of the King (things like watching R-rated movies, wearing skimpy clothes, cursing, lying, and gossiping).

And instead of the popularity and applause that usually accompanies nobility, we can expect to suffer some slings (being mocked or dissed for our beliefs) and arrows (being rejected by girls who think we're goody two-shoes).

What's more, we'll have to do battle with the King's arch enemy, Satan, for sure. This will often leave us feeling dejected, shunned, bullied, bruised, and despised. Our saving grace, though, is that our Brother, Jesus, has been through all this already. The world hated him first, and he overcame it (John 15:18, 16:33). So he can help us overcome our hardships, too.

The Bible says if we suffer with Jesus, we will also share in his glory (Romans 8:17). So if we bear our injustices in the same spirit Jesus bore his, then we'll be united with Him in getting the same reward: The keys to his kingdom.

And not only will we receive our inheritance, but we'll also get a seat of honor among the majesties of heaven. "Those who are victorious will sit with me on my throne," Jesus says, "just as I was victorious and sat with my Father on his throne" (Revelation 3:21 NLT).

Whoa! Think of it: As his princess-daughters, we'll be able to live for all eternity among the royals of heaven—our Heavenly Father, the King of Kings; our Savior, Jesus Christ; the Helper, God's Holy Spirit; and all the saints. What's more, we'll have the joyful privilege of seeing God "as he is" (1 John 3:2) and the honor of being able to lovingly call him "Abba Father" (Romans 8:15 NLT).

Food for Thought

Girls who wear "princess" on their backpacks (and yup, on their bums) would rather be pawns of the world than daughters of the King. Let's pray they come to know their Father soon.

Second Thoughts

Princesses of the world may have lots. But the Bible says that in your wildest dreams, you can't even imagine what God has planned for you (1 Corinthians 2:9).

Divine Thoughts

Heavenly Father, thank you for making me your princess-daughter. Help me to act in ways that always make you proud. Amen.

Your Thoughts:

Devotion 30

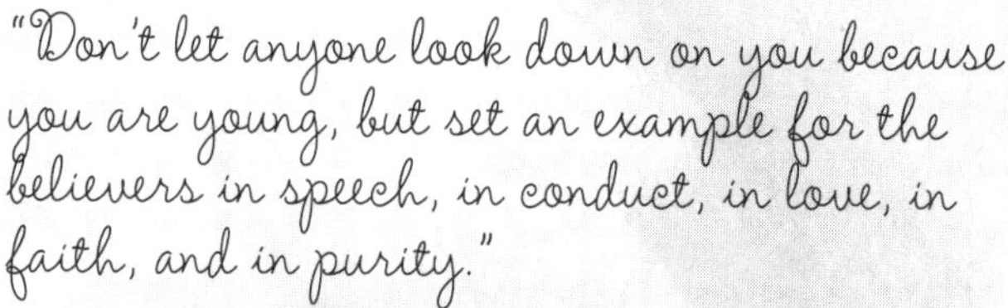

1 Timothy 4:12

You're Never Too Young

Fed up with hearing, "She's just a kid. What can *she* do?"

Don't give it a second thought. Keep this in mind instead: The Bible says, "Stay true to what is right for the sake of your own salvation and the salvation of those who hear you" (1 Timothy 4:16 NLT). So no matter how old we are, if our hearts are willing, God can work though us to do incredible things.

Take Moses's sister, Miriam. Her unselfish actions and quick thinking reunited her mom with her brother and saved Moses to deliver God's people from slavery. How old was she? Your age—between 7 and 12.

Then there's Esther. When an evil official ordered the slaughter of the Jews, as queen, Esther was the only person in a position to help. Problem was her husband, the king, forbade anyone to approach him without being summoned.

But there was no time to wait. So Esther prayed and fasted, then risked her life by going to the king for help. Her noble act saved her people from getting wiped out. When did she do this? In her teens.

Yes, then there was one extremely noble, young girl, Mary (estimated age 12-14), who answered, "I am the Lord's servant. May everything you have said about me come true" (Luke 1:38 NLT) to usher in the Savior of the world to our rescue.

Okay, so we may never get to serve like Miriam, Esther, or Mary. But we *can* do something incredibly noble every day—something Paul suggested to Timothy when he sent him to preach to early Christians. We can be a perfect, pure-hearted witness, a girl who shows the world by her words and actions what it means to be a follower of Christ (1 Timothy 4:12). We can act and speak and treat others in a way that'll have people saying, "If this is what being a Christian is like ... I want in."

A little girl at the mall did that recently. When a teenager yelled and cussed an elderly sales clerk, the youngster said to her mom in a voice all could hear, "I don't think that girlie better talk to someone's Grannie like that. God doesn't like it." She was around five.

So, it doesn't matter how old we are. If we accept God into our lives, he can use us in all *sorts* of ways.

Food for Thought

God uses tweens regularly for awesome things, like walking for cancer or giving witness talks. Have a idea for furthering God's kingdom? Start organizing.

Second Thoughts

God used teen boys to further his plans, too. David slew the giant; Josiah got rid of idol worship; and a little boy shared his lunch and became part of a miracle.

Divine Thoughts

Heavenly Father, I may be young, but I'm all yours. Use me to let others come to you. Amen.

Your Thoughts:

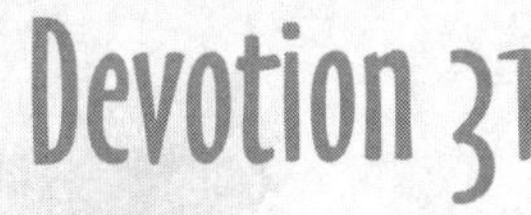

Devotion 31

"Honor your father and your mother, as the Lord your God commanded you."

Deuteronomy 5:16 NLT

The Good Daughter

Nobility puts a lot of emphasis on *who* our parents are. But the Whatever life puts the focus on *how* we treat them—which should always be with honor and respect. God feels so strongly about this, he's made "Honor your father and mother" one of his Top Ten Rules (Exodus 20:12).

See, our moms and dads are sort of like God's representatives here on earth, taking care of us, loving us, and making sure we're headed in the right direction—towards him. God gives parents this huge responsibility, but he also holds them accountable for the job they do. So if we want our moms and dads to get high marks, we should do everything we can to make their work as our parents easier.

Okay, okay, so we understand parents can drive a girl up the wall sometimes. And we know, sometimes, it's, like, way hard to hold them in high esteem when we think they're over-protective, old-fashioned, grumpy, stubborn, and impatient. Why should we?

Because honoring our parents isn't based on whether we feel like it, or whether we think they deserve it. It's based on obeying what God has commanded (Deuteronomy 5:16). And it's based on the part our mother and father play in giving us the most precious thing we have: life. So, even if they never did another thing, that would be reason enough to honor them.

But we all know the giving doesn't stop there. Most parents do a gazillion things for us—feed us, give us a place to live, support the family, take care of our bodily and spiritual well-being, taxi us everywhere, find money for clothes and stuff, celebrate holidays and birthdays, put up with our moods. We could go on, but we'd run out of space.

And many times, we're so focused on what parents are not doing and giving us, we take all this good stuff for granted.

Okay, so back to the honoring. How do we do that? It's kind of obvious what we shouldn't do—no flippant "Whatevers," no rolling our eyes, ignoring, interrupting, whining, or arguing. What we *can* do is listen, obey, be cheerful, address parents respectfully, help out, and show our love by acting in a way that reflects we're part of a God-focused family.

Above all, we can honor our parents by praying for them and asking God to bless them.

Food for Thought

BTW, the Fifth Commandment comes with a promise: "If you honor your father and mother, 'things will go well for you'" (Ephesians 6:3 NLT).

Second Thoughts

In Bible times, there were harsh consequences for sons and daughters who disrespected their parents. Read about it in Deuteronomy 21:18-21; Exodus 21:15, 17.

Divine Thoughts

Dear Lord, sometimes I'm so wrapped up in myself, I take my parents for granted. Help me to always be grateful and honor them as I honor you. Amen.

Your Thoughts:

"Do not seek revenge or bear a grudge against anyone among your people, but love your neighbor as yourself. I am the LORD."

Leviticus 19:18

Forgiving: It "Ain't" Easy

"Think this dress would work?" Barbara asked Margie. "I could be a Lady in Waiting."

"Nah, makes you look fat," Margie said. So the two of them left the mall.

Then, on the night of Vicki's Medieval Theme Party, Margie walks in, and everyone oohs and ahhs her outfit. Barbara takes one look and her mouth drops. There's Margie ... in the Lady in Waiting dress! Arghhhhh! Barbara is so angry she could spit. When Margie comes over to talk, Barbara walks away. *I'll get her back if it's the last thing I do,* she thinks. Then she sits fuming, planning her revenge.

Okay, so what Margie did stinks. But will acting crummy back solve anything? Nope. In fact, taking revenge is always a lose-lose situation: It hurts God and the person you're trying to get "even" with, but most of all, it hurts you. Holding on to evil eats away at your heart and makes you do stupid (and sinful) things. And a nah-nah-nah-nah-nah attitude is petty and childish.

The Bible says, "Don't let evil get the best of you; get the best of evil by doing good" (Romans 12:21 MSG). How? Join forces with Jesus to stop evil cold using the best weapon there is: Forgiveness.

Okay, you totally don't want to. But one look at the cross shows you why you have to: Jesus forgave you. So you have to "make allowance" and be "quick to forgive an offense" (Colossians 3:13 NLT, MSG).

Forgiving is not only noble, it's smart. It shows God you understand the message of the cross and you're willing to copy it. What's more, it frees you to accept the wrong you suffered, get over it, and get your mind on happier thoughts.

Another reason to let go? The Bible says God's justice will take care of deciding what's wrong and what should be done about it. And the wording couldn't be clearer: "Never take revenge. Leave that to the righteous anger of God" (Romans 12:19 NLT).

But, hey, here's something you *can* do that'll floor the girl you're upset with: "surprise [her] with goodness" (Romans 12:20 MSG). Being nice to someone who has been crummy to you can make her think twice about what she's done, feel sorry, and maybe do the right thing the next time.

So forgiving actually lets God make something good out of something bad. You just have to do your part.

Food for Thought

When you forgive, you're not saying, "Oh, what you did was fine. No problem." You're just trying to love the person in spite of what he or she did.

Second Thoughts

Read about the king who had mercy and the servant who had none in Matthew 18:21-35. How does this story make you feel?

Divine Thoughts

Dearest Jesus, sometimes, I really want to get even with people. So please give me an extra helping of your grace to be forgiving like you. Amen.

Your Thoughts:

Section 4

Whatever's Right

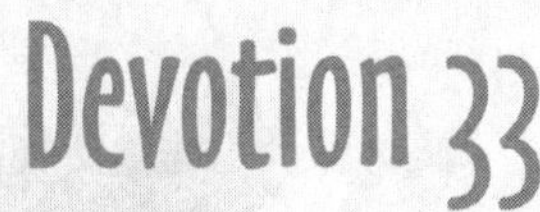

"The path of life leads upward for the wise; they leave the grave behind."

Proverbs 15:24 NLT

The Narrow Road

Celia and Abby were hiking in the park when they came to a fork in the road. "Which way, Abby?" Celia asked. "I have, like, no clue."

"Let's take this one," Abby replied.

"And that would be because?" Celia asked.

"Well, it's wide and you can see it's pretty worn. So lots of people must have gone that way. The other path is narrow and thick with bushes."

The wide, much-traveled road might be best if we're hiking. But if we're trying to find God's home, the Bible says the narrow road's definitely the way to go (Matthew 7:13).

This tiny path may seem tough traveling at first. It will have ruts and thorny bushes and may be so overgrown, we could easily miss it. Still, if the Bible says it's the only road that leads to heaven, once we find it, the important thing is to stick with it and not get detoured.

Even with rough spots, the narrow path's better because it has 24/7 assistance from an expert guide: God. And if we wander off the road to the right or the left, the Bible says, "your ears will hear a voice behind you, saying, 'This is the way; walk in it'" (Isaiah 30:21).

But wait, the wide road is a gas the world tells us. And it's way exciting, too. On it, we can text gossip instead of studying, go to R-rated movies, and do lots of other cool stuff.

Oh, and the toll on this road's half nothing, the world swears. The price? God's disappointment, poor grades, lost friends, and arguments with parents, at the most. As for heaven, it's a long ways off, the wide-roaders tell us. So "have fun now," they say. "Join us on our sup-pah highway."

As if.

The Bible says, "For wide is the gate and broad is the road that leads to destruction, and many enter through it" (Matthew 7:13). But we aren't looking to go in that direction. We'll stick with the rugged, narrow road. And if we stumble onto one of those forks, we won't freak. We'll turn to God and say, "Show me the right path, O Lord; point out the road for me to follow" (Psalm 25:4), and we'll be golden ... back on the narrow road again.

Food for Thought

Estimates are that Jesus traveled about 15-25 miles a day, and in his 33 years, a rough total of 21,525. (He must have worn out a lot of sandals.)

Second Thoughts

Make close friends with other girls who are traveling the narrow road. This way you can share experiences and watch out for each other.

Divine Thoughts

Dearest Jesus, a gazillion times a day I'm at that fork in the road, and I have to make a choice. Please help me make the right one. Amen.

Your Thoughts:

Devotion 34

"If you love only those who love you, what reward is there for that? Even corrupt tax collectors do that much."

Matthew 5:46 NLT

Loving the Queen of Mean

True or false? There are some people who are, like, just plain awful, and there's nothing you can do about it.

False. You can always do something about nasty people—though it's probably the very last thing you want to do. You can love them.

Blah, you think. *Love the queen of mean?* (Let's just call her Gail.) *She's loud and obnoxious; she's always making fun of me. Why would I ever want to love her?*

Because our Lord asked you to—because he showed you how—and because he'll help you do it, if you ask.

See, Jesus is big on love. Everything he does and asks you to do is based on it. The Bible consistently tells us to love one another (1 Thessalonians 4:9; 1 John 2:8; 3:11, 23; 4:7; 2 John 1, 6). The Ten Commandments all stem from the first two that focus on love. Love is how people recognize us as Christians. So if you say you love Jesus, you gotta love others. That's all there is to it.

Loving just your BFF or your good friends won't cut it, though. Jesus knows that's a cinch. The hard part is loving the Gails of the world. "But I say love your enemies!" Jesus said. "Pray for those who persecute you!" (Matthew 5:44 NLT).

But Jesus didn't just give us this command and then say "Go figure."

He demonstrated what it meant by his own life. He was accused falsely. People made fun of him, hit and whipped him. His enemies spit on him and put a crown of spiky thorns on his head. They made him carry a humongous cross; they nailed him to it. And he still loved them.

Think about that when you're faced with a girl who calls you names, or dumps you for someone more popular. Why? Because Jesus went through horrible things—and still loved. And he expects us to follow his lead.

To do this, we may have to die a little to our own feelings—of jealousy, anger, distrust—so that the Jesus in us can take over, grow stronger, and love through us.

God knows loving the unloveables may be like mission impossible for us, but not for him. He also doesn't expect you to do this alone. So ask him to send you an extra helping of grace. Remember, with God, all things are possible (Mark 10:27) ... even loving the queen of mean. Fact is you gotta love everybody, and with God's help, you can.

Food for Thought

How do we love others? We include them. We try to find things we have in common. (Cats? Cooking? Scrapbooking?) We don't call them clueless behind their backs.

Second Thoughts

When Jesus says love one another, it doesn't mean you have to love their bad behavior. Love the image of God in them.

Divine Thoughts

Heavenly Father, teach me to love like Jesus so I can love everyone, even people I don't like. Amen.

Your Thoughts:

Devotion 35

"I praise you because I am fearfully and wonderfully made."

Psalm 139:14

Who's "Just Right"? You Are

Latoya was babysitting the twins when their sister, an irresistibly cute toddler named Louisa, crawled to the crib and pulled herself up.

"Yo, girls," she gurgled in baby talk. "Do these diapers make me look fat?"

Yeah, we're pulling your leg. But God could view us as just as silly when we obsess about our weight, our looks, and our clothes.

Okay, we know God made us amazing. The Bible says so. He patterned us after himself, so we have to be (Genesis 1:27). We're awesome creatures with bodies that can walk, talk, taste, think, feel, and make choices. We can play the piano, run a marathon, become President ... if we've a mind to.

But our insecurity will paint us a different picture. When we look in the mirror, it will taunt us: "You don't measure up," it'll whisper. "Your bum is gi-normous in these jeans," it'll say critically. "You have no shape at all. You look like a boy. Your legs are like logs. You're one ugly chick."

Says who? Certainly not God. He loves us unconditionally. He takes us "as is." And he wants us to love ourselves that way as well. When we do, we're less likely to go overboard dieting, exercising, and primping in the hopes of reaching some unrealistic goal the world tells us we're falling short of.

Because if we're busy trying to turn ourselves into pencil-thin fashionistas, we have less time for what's really important: honoring God by buffing up our inner selves.

See, God doesn't judge us—like the world does—on our outward appearance. He looks inside at our hearts. So we ought to "Cultivate inner beauty, the gentle, gracious kind that God delights in" (1 Peter 3:4 MSG). That doesn't mean we don't try to look our best and wear nice clothes, or that we don't exercise and eat right. It just means we shouldn't be so excessively focused on our physical selves that we let our spiritual selves go to pot.

Okay, so how do we get gorgeous spiritually? Let's see. We could soften our souls with the cream of kindness, lose the weight of anger with a diet of forgiveness, and dress up our hearts in a designer outfit of love, for starters.

Then we could practice ignoring those little voices and try becoming as beautiful in our own eyes as we are in God's.

Food for Thought

Jesus was "just right" to his Father, but as for the world's view, "There was nothing attractive about him, nothing to cause us to take a second look" (Isaiah 53:2 MSG).

Second Thoughts

Remind yourself of your "awesomeness." Tack up notes on your mirrors that read: "GOD MADE ME AMAZING."

Divine Thoughts

Dearest God, please help me to stop being insecure about my body. In Jesus's name, I pray. Amen.

Your Thoughts:

Devotion 36

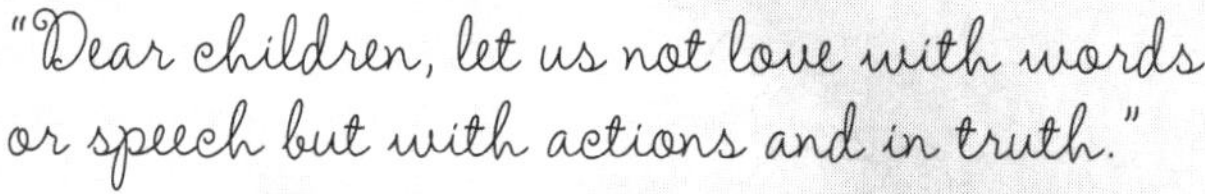
"Dear children, let us not love with words or speech but with actions and in truth."

1 John 3:18

Be an Action Hero

We all know girls who are all talk but no action. They yak about saving the environment, but don't volunteer for school clean-up projects. They say, "Let's start a soup kitchen garden," but never mention it again.

How does that make you feel? Disappointed, for sure.

That's how God feels when girls say they're Christians, but don't show it in the things they do—especially in how they treat others.

The Bible says, "If people say they have faith, but do nothing, their faith is worth nothing." In the same way, "Faith by itself—that does nothing—is dead" (James 2:14, 17 NCV).

A lunchroom incident involving a girl named Maribel is the perfect example. Maribel wore her cross proudly and said grace before she ate meals. But when faced with a big-time opportunity to witness by putting her faith into practice in the "doing good to others" department, she failed miserably.

Maribel's mom fixed her a huge lunch. She was about to chow down, when she noticed a girl from her class sitting reading a magazine, no food in sight. She overheard this girl tell someone she'd left her backpack on the bus. But word was that the girl's father had lost his job. So she might not have had lunch in the first place.

Instead of offering to share, Maribel blew the girl off. "Someone else will give her something," she said to her BFF, Alyson. "Besides, I'm starving."

Poof! Gone was Maribel's follow-through from saying grace. Gone was her chance to act on God's commandment to love others as ourselves.

Alyson, on the other hand, rose to the occasion. She quickly brought her lunch over to the girl and sat down. "Hey," she said. "My mom made this monster sandwich. Share it with me, please, or I'll explode."

With one gesture, Alyson became the "action hero of the day," a girl who doesn't just go through the motions of being a Christian, but one who talks the talk *and* walks (in love, with Jesus) the walk. Let's you and I be "action" heroes today, too. Okay?

Food for Thought

Sometimes YOU are the answer to someone's prayer. Proverbs says, "Never walk away from someone who deserves help; your hand is God's hand for that person" (Proverbs 3:27 MSG).

Second Thoughts

There are lots of needy families. You could say, "Oh, well, what can I do?" Or you could, if you're not already involved in a food drive, organize one.

Divine Thoughts

Jesus, thank you for the chance to not only talk about loving my neighbor, but also to show that love by the way I act. Amen.

Your Thoughts:

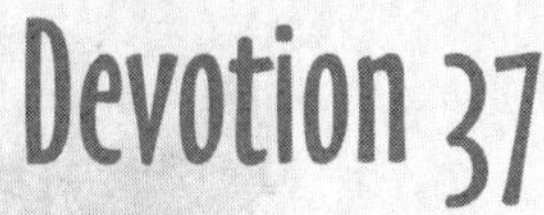

Devotion 37

"Give to everyone what you owe them ... respect and honor to those who are in authority."

Romans 13:7 NLT

A Little R.E.S.P.E.C.T.

Miss Toilsome asks Jenny to stop texting and put away her phone.

"Two minutes, Teach," Jenny says without looking up. "I just need to finish this one tiny message, and I'm, like, done. There, now, I'm all yours."

Girls at their desks start to snigger.

There's no place for disrespect in the Whatever girl's lifestyle, because when we disrespect people who've been put in charge, we disrespect God.

And that includes teachers. The Bible says, "There is no authority except from God [by His permission, his sanction], and those that exist do so by God's appointment" (Romans 13:1 AMP). So God has appointed specific teachers to have authority over us for specific reasons, and he wants us to treat them as though he himself were teaching the class.

Even if we think the teacher's lame? Yup. Even if we think she's picking on us? Yup. Peter told Christian slaves to respect and obey both the nice *and* the cruel masters. He told them to be polite and not to talk back. He said, "What counts is that you put up with it for God's sake when you're treated badly for no good reason" (1 Peter 2:19 MSG). He told them if they did, God would greatly bless them. On the other hand, Paul warned, "whoever rebels against the authority is rebelling against what God has instituted," and those who do will be punished (Romans 13:2).

See, we don't have the whole picture, so we don't know what God has up his sleeve. Maybe he sent a certain teacher our way, not only so we can learn, say, math or science, but also so we can learn patience, obedience, kindness, and perseverance—important values that'll help us get along in the real world. Then, too, perhaps *you* have been sent to that particular teacher so he can learn some of the same things.

For sure, a little respect goes a long way. So let's start today. Here's how:

- ♥ Listen and pay attention in class. Don't act up for attention. Don't make jokes at the teacher's expense.
- ♥ Say, "Thank you," and "Please," and call the teacher by her full name.
- ♥ Help teachers pass out papers or carry supplies. Hold the door open.
- ♥ Be on time to class and with assignments.

Remember, girls who show respect will always win out—in this world and more importantly in the next.

Food for Thought

The Bible says, "Show proper respect to everyone" (1 Peter 2:17). That means little brothers and sisters, your peers, the cafeteria ladies ... *everyone.*

Second Thoughts

If someone in authority asks you to do something that's not in accordance with God's laws, you obviously can't do it. But you can explain why in a respectful way.

Divine Thoughts

Dearest Jesus, remind me that being a teacher isn't the easiest of jobs and I may not be the easiest girl to teach. Amen.

Your Thoughts:

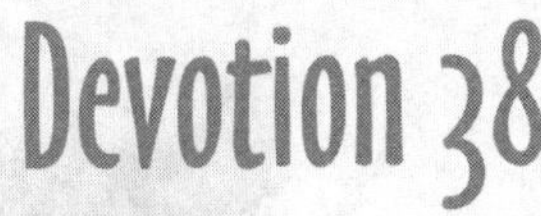

Devotion 38

*"My flesh and my heart may fail,
but God is the strength of my heart
and my portion forever."*

Psalm 73:26

Got God? Got Everything

It just doesn't seem right. Everywhere we look, girls are practically getting away with murder. They cheat and get good marks. They're snotty to teachers and never get punished. They're stuck-up, yet still popular.

What's wrong with this picture? You gotta wonder.

Back in David's time, a man named Asaph (a talented music director in the Temple) was way bummed about this. So he wrote up his experience in a psalm (73).

Asaph believed that God is good, and yet he admits that for a time, he "nearly" lost faith in how God operates.

Simply put, he complained: "God, these wicked guys don't follow your rules and they prosper. Me? I behave, but have nothing to show for it. What good is being good? Phooey!" (Psalm 73:4-13).

Now, Asaph felt that way because he did something we all do sometimes: He took his eyes off God and put them on himself. And the more he thought about what he perceived was his unfair treatment, the more jealous and disgusted he became. He felt confused, but didn't know what to do.

"When I tried to understand all this," he wrote in the psalm, "it troubled me deeply till I entered the sanctuary of God; then I understood their final destiny. Surely you place them on slippery ground; you cast them down to ruin" (Psalm 73:16-18).

Returning to God's house snapped Asaph out of his self-pity. Away from worldly distractions, he was better able to reconnect with the Lord and receive the grace to refocus on the truth he knew from the start: God is good.

We can almost see him smacking his palm to his forehead, thinking, *What a dummy I've been. I might not have as many riches as the wicked, but I'm way better off because of what I do have: the Lord.*

"Whom have I in heaven but you?" Asaph wrote in this "ah-ha" moment. "And earth has nothing I desire besides you" (Psalm 73:25).

After that, Asaph admitted he'd been wrong to complain and marveled that, even then, God still loved and guided him. With that came joy and praise. "As for me," he wrote in the psalm's last lines, "it is good to be near God. I have made the Sovereign Lord my refuge; I will tell of all your deeds" (Psalms 73:28).

Lesson learned: Wealth and success can be here today and gone tomorrow. But when you've got God, you have everything.

Food for Thought

Feeling whiney? Read Psalm 73. Then go talk to the Lord and listen for his reply. When you're finished, do what Asaph did: Tell everyone, "God is good."

Second Thoughts

Asaph and his fellow musicians sang worship songs and played praise music in the Temple. What's your favorite Christian band?

Divine Thoughts

Heavenly Father, when I see others who do wrong and seem to get away with it, help me remember Asaph. Amen.

Your Thoughts:

Devotion 39

"There is a time for everything,
and a season for every activity under heaven."

Ecclesiastes 3:1

The Hands on God's Clock

Tick, tock. Tick, tock. Tick, tock.

Thinking about time can drive us crazy—especially when we're waiting for something. We're anxious and impatient. So we pray, "God, can you work faster, pa-leese? I love you. Hurry. Bye."

Though our prayers may be sincere and we believe God hears them, there's one tiny problem: God's plans unfold according to his timetable, not ours. What's more, the hands on his clock are way different. Whereas we see only what's going on minute by minute, the Bible says, "A thousand years in [God's] sight are like a day that has just gone by" (Psalm 90:4).

It's a common mistake, though—thinking God operates on Earth Standard Time. Even Bible heroes like God's friend Abraham and his wife, Sarah, had these issues.

God promised Abraham he'd have a huge family. But when Sarah reached ninety and had no children, she lost faith. (She forgot who she was dealing with.) So, she took matters into her own hands. As was the custom then, she gave her slave, Hagar, to Abraham as a surrogate wife. Hagar had a son, and this caused bad feelings all around, but mostly for Sarah. Then God delivered on his promise, and Sarah, "bore a son to Abraham in his old age, *at the very time* God had promised him" (Genesis 21:1–2, emphasis added).

Abraham wondered himself when he'd become a dad. Yet his faith was so strong, that even though he didn't know *how* God was going to deliver his promise, Abraham believed that God *would.* And he was rewarded.

God wants us to have faith like Abraham, because he's not always going to give us what we want right away. And he has his reasons. Maybe the waiting is to test our faith, or to teach us a lesson. Or maybe it's because giving us what we want would put us in harm's or sin's way.

Whatever it is, let's trust that God knows best, and that timing, in his hands, is always perfect. And when we pray, instead of "Hurry, Lord," let's copy the psalmist who, with humility and patience, said, "I pray to you, Lord. *So when the time is right,* answer me and help me with your wonderful love" (Psalm 69:13 CEV, emphasis added).

Food for Thought

When a decision looms, don't make yourself nutzy over timing, but rather ask God to direct your steps. Then let go. For more, read Psalm 37:23.

Second Thoughts

Remember timing's important at home, too. Don't spring things on your parents when they're busy. Wait, and you'll probably get a better response.

Divine Thoughts

Dear Lord, I hate to wait. Please send your Helper to teach me patience, so I can trust that everything's happening as it should. Amen.

Your Thoughts:

Devotion 40

"Keep a close watch on how you live and on your teaching. Stay true to what is right for the sake of your own salvation and the salvation of those who hear you."

1 Timothy 4:16 NLT

Do the Right Thing

Jean and her friends were having lunch at the local diner. The place was jammed and the waitress was frazzled. Daniella came late and ordered fries and a coke. When the bill came, her meal wasn't on it.

"Don't be a wuss, Dee," Jean said. "It was her fault. And she was, like, a total witch. Let's just go."

"Nah," Dee said. "I ate the food; I gotta pay."

Doing what's right may not be the easiest, coolest, or most popular thing. But if we love God and are trying to live the Whatever life, we have to do what's right: We have to keep God's commandments—no ifs, ands, or buts.

The Bible says we can expect a bunch of benefits for doing the right thing.

The flip side of this is if we know what's right and don't do it, we're sinning. We can't excuse or worm our way out.

Right living has to be a 24/7 priority. We have to say "No" to the devil's lies, like, "It's okay this time." We can't listen to the world's lie, "This used to be wrong, but it's not anymore."

David did the right thing by Saul, his enemy—not once—but twice. On two separate occasions, David could have killed him. But David knew it wasn't his place to harm the king God had anointed. So both times, he let Saul live.

Okay, but even David—who loved God a lot—slipped up and sinned with Bathsheba. Then he tried to brush it under the rug. Problem was, he couldn't. Not admitting his sins made David weak and miserable. He was worn out from groaning all day (Psalm 32:3). So, he confessed his sins and begged God's forgiveness. When he did, he said, "Suddenly, the pressure was gone—my guilt dissolved, my sin disappeared" (Psalms 32:5 MSG).

So the good news is God blesses us when we do the right thing in the first place. The even-better news is if we mess up, admit we're wrong, and tell God we're sorry, he will take us back and put everything right again (1 John 1:9 TLB).

Food for Thought

Good news: Jesus said those who are insulted for his sake can expect a reward in heaven (Matthew 5:11–12).

Second Thoughts

A Whatever girl can be trusted to do the right thing no matter where she is and who she's with. Is that you?

Divine Thoughts

Dearest Jesus, it's hard to do the right thing when I know others will make fun of me. But with your grace, I can. Amen.

Your Thoughts:

Devotion 41

"Do everything without complaining or arguing."

Philippians 2:14

A New Attitude

"Wow, that routine was, like, awesome," Janice said to her BFF after cheerleading practice.

"It stunk," Mary Lou said. "The new coach was lame. And what a pukey green color uniform. I mean, really, couldn't they do *any* better?"

It's torture being around a complainer. All we want to do is make them stop. No matter what they're talking about, they're always criticizing.

So it's a good idea to listen to ourselves regularly to make sure *we* aren't whiners, too.

Grumbling makes God angry. Open the Bible to Exodus for the proof. God saved his people from slavery, and what did he hear? "Where's the water?" the Israelites griped. "We hate that white stuff (manna). Give us meat. Are we there yet?" (Exodus 16:1-36; 17:1-7 paraphrased).

God's answer? "Because you have complained against me every one of you who is twenty years old or older ... will die" (Numbers 14:29 NLT). Yikes!

Okay, you're thinking, *But, I don't complain against God. It's just that gross cafeteria food.*

Wrong! Anytime you whine about anything, you're aiming that barb at God ... because God gives us everything. So you're as much as telling him, "This just isn't up to my standards, God. I deserve better."

"You must have the same attitude that Christ Jesus had" (Philippians 2:5 NLT), the Bible says, and Jesus wasn't a griper. He accepted the good and the bad equally in total obedience to the will of his Father.

When he was dead tired and wanted some quiet, he didn't complain, "Heal me. Heal me. Can't these people give it a rest?" And when the little children came to see him, Jesus didn't pout: "That's all I need—a bunch of kids climbing all over me."

Nope. On both occasions, Jesus was humble, open, and loving. His attitude was "What can I do for them?" not "What are they doing to me?"

So how do we get a Christ-like attitude?

- ♥ ***Be thankful:*** Concentrate on the grace God has showered on you. If the food isn't great when you eat out, think about girls who can't afford to go out at all ... even to a Micky D's.

- ***Be humble:*** Remember Jesus, the King of the world, didn't expect the best. He was accepting and never made a fuss.
- ***Be satisfied:*** Paul learned to be okay with whatever came his way (Philippians 4:11–13). Try it. It's a great attitude to have.

Food for Thought

Complaining never gets you anywhere. Jonah protested about going to Nineveh. He wound up in a big fish, then had to go to Nineveh anyway (Jonah 1-4).

Second Thoughts

Cut down on complaints by thinking Whatever thoughts that are true, noble, right, pure, lovely, admirable, excellent, or praiseworthy.

Divine Thoughts

Jesus, help me to have the right attitude about things—a "no complaints" attitude, so I can be more like you. Amen.

Your Thoughts:

Section 5

Whatever's Pure

Devotion 42

"Keep your eyes open, hold tight to your convictions, give it all you've got, be resolute, and love without stopping."

1 Corinthians 16:13 MSG

One Hundred Percent Pure You

"Look," Nancy said to her BFF, "I didn't know what the video was about when Stacey asked me over. I can't back out now."

"I did," Emily said. "I just told her I don't do R movies."

"And she probably thinks you're dork of the day," Nancy said and walked off.

One of the hardest things about growing up is finding out who we are and what we believe ... and then sticking to it.

If you're striving to be like Jesus, that means you've got to be true to God, to his Word, and to your beliefs. It means you don't become a people pleaser at the expense of your faith. You don't make decisions based on what's popular. You don't say you believe one thing one minute, then act like you don't the next.

Being true to yourself means honoring the voice of the Holy Spirit inside you. It means having values and holding on to them even though others make fun of you or treat you like you have atomic B.O.

Jesus was awesome at this. He aligned his will with God's and didn't waver.

He didn't stop eating with sinners because people whispered behind his back.

He didn't take up a sword because people wanted a military leader.

He didn't lie about who he was to save his life.

Jesus was the real thing through and through.

You can be that way, too. But it's going to take courage. You need to be one strong cookie to be "God's Girl," instead of "At-the-Mercy-of-Anybody's-Whim-Because-She-Wants-to-Be-Liked-Girl."

For starters, try writing a manifesto (a statement of your intentions) describing who you are and what you believe. Something like, "I'm Jean. I'm a Christian tween who believes a loving God saw me in his mind before the world began, and created me to be exactly who I am, a special person dedicated just to him.

"What's more, I refuse to be anyone other than who I am, and who I am doesn't get involved with stuff that I'd be ashamed of before God."

Mapping out your identity as a child of God can help you remain true to him and yourself. It reminds you of what's really important: responding to the Lord's love, not pressure from girls who may like you today but not tomorrow.

Oh, and if anyone puts her hands on her hips and says, "And just who do you think YOU are?" you'll know exactly how to answer.

Food for Thought

Being your own person doesn't mean you block everyone else out. It just means you listen, then decide what to do based on what God would want you to do.

Second Thoughts

In war lingo, "stick to your guns" meant a soldier would stand and keep shooting even though it would put him in harm's way. Do you "stick to your guns" when it comes to your beliefs?

Divine Thoughts

Jesus, people always knew where you stood—with your Father—in everything. Help me to be true to myself by being true to you. Amen.

Your Thoughts:

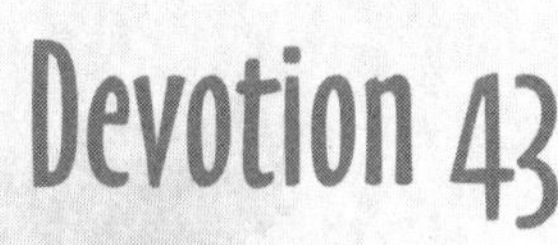

Devotion 43

"Run from anything that stimulates youthful lusts. Instead, pursue righteous living, faithfulness, love, and peace. Enjoy the companionship of those who call on the Lord with pure hearts."

2 Timothy 2:22 NLT

Making Tracks

Chloe and her little brother, Jason, were watching TV when a "girl-gets-guy-because-she-uses-ABC-mouthwash" ad came on, and the model was in the process of planting a kiss on her newly acquired boyfriend.

Jason grabbed a pillow, ran to the TV, and covered the screen to hide what he called "that schmushy love stuff."

Poor Jason would be a pretty busy little boy, though, if he had to run and cover up all the "schmushy love stuff" around today. Because there's scads of it—almost everywhere—as advertisers use sex to try to sell almost everything. You can't even watch TV or a movie anymore without something offensive embarrassing you. And speaking of TV and movies, there are way too many storylines that suggest loose morals and binge drinking are the norm and perfectly acceptable.

Okay, so you obviously can't get rid of all this. But you can limit your exposure. The Bible says, "turn from godless living and sinful pleasures. We should live in this evil world with wisdom, righteousness, and devotion to God" (Titus 2:12 NLT).

These tips could help:

- If you see something, say something. Many girls sit through gross stuff—stuff they don't even want to see—because they're afraid to speak up. So be the one to say "Nah" if someone suggests watching anything violent or improper.
- Check Christian websites for book, movie, and music reviews that list clean, fun entertainment. There are plenty of things out there that are interesting, cool, and fun to watch and listen to that won't pollute your thoughts.
- If you find yourself somewhere where others tempt you to go on inappropriate websites or chat sites, let your feet do the talking. Say "adios" and split.
- Delete gross photos or jokes from your computer or mobile devices ASAP, and tell the sender to please stop forwarding stuff like that.
- Finally, hang with girls who love Jesus. You'll find, like you, they'd rather fill their minds with Whatever—true, lovely, noble, admirable, excellent, pure stuff—instead of junk.

Surround yourself with girls like this, and there will be no need for anyone to hold up a pillow for you.

Food for Thought

Joseph refused the advances of his boss's wife, Mrs. Potiphar. Because he loved God too much, he made tracks. He didn't walk—he ran—out the door (Genesis 39:12).

Second Thoughts

The Bible says, "a young person can stay pure by obeying your [God's] word and following its rules" (Psalm 119:9 NLT).

Divine Thoughts

Dearest Jesus, help me turn away from the offensive stuff that's all around, and keep my thoughts focused on you. Amen.

Your Thoughts:

Devotion 44

"Since the Master honors you with a body, honor him with your body!"

1 Corinthians 6:13 MSG

On Loan

When God made us in an amazing way, when he knit our bodies together in our mother's womb, he had a purpose for those bodies—to serve, glorify, and be joined with him in heaven for eternity. Satan tricked us into sinning and tried to steal us away. But God sent Jesus to redeem us, to buy us at "a high price" (1 Corinthians 7:23 NLT) with the blood of his cross.

So, guess what? "Your own body does not belong to you" (1 Corinthians 6:19 TLB).

See, God gives us these bodies on loan, for our temporary use, and since they're not ours, we have to be careful about what happens to them. As caretakers, we constantly have to think about where our bodies are going and what they're doing, as someday we'll have to make an accounting to the real owner: God.

What's more, we have to take charge of our bodies, not let them take charge of us. We can't use the excuse some girls do, "Oh, I couldn't control myself," because if we can't control our own selves, who can?

And keeping them pure is a big part of that, because as Paul told the Corinthians, "No other sin so clearly affects the body as this one does. For sexual immorality is a sin against your own body" (1 Corinthians 6:18 NLT).

That's where the Whatever test comes in: We can ask ourselves, "Is what I'm taking part in—what I'm reading, looking at, listening to—something uplifting? Beneficial? Is it noble, right, pure, lovely, admirable, excellent, or praiseworthy? If not, then it's not for me."

See, God didn't just make our bodies so we could enjoy pleasurable things like pepperoni pizzas, magnificent sunsets, and a holy marriage union. He also made them to be—

- ♥ A vehicle to get us from A (earth) to B (heaven)
- ♥ A temple where his Spirit can live
- ♥ The seed from which he'll create our improved eternal bodies
- ♥ A mirror to reflect his light and love

So if we use our bodies for his purposes, and keep our own desires in check, his glory will shine through us and others will see just how totally amazing he is.

Food for Thought

Your value is not based on how you look to that cute boy in your class, but how you look to God. And if you keep yourself pure, you'll look awesome!

Second Thoughts

Taking care of your body with good food, exercise, and proper hygiene shows that you respect who's living inside: God's Spirit.

Divine Thoughts

Lord, help me to keep my body clean and pure inside and out. Amen.

Your Thoughts:

Devotion 45

"I will not set before my eyes anything that is base."
Psalm 101:3 NRSV

Heard the One About . . .

Denisha was showing her mom the cooking blog she designed, when a "flagged" message from a volleyball teammate popped into her email. When she opened it, there was an obscene picture with a crude caption.

"Junk mail," she said to her mom, hiding her embarrassment and quickly deleting it.

A lot of coarse jokes and photos make the rounds as Internet humor and wind up as messages on our computers, tablets, and phones. They're often sent by acquaintances or even BFFs who aren't thinking things through—people who feel these things are so way funny, they just have to share.

Problem with this stuff is it's masquerading as something harmless, when it really isn't. "Oh, come on," girls will say. "It's just a joke. You'll ROTFLOL." These people firmly believe that. But with so much crudeness around and everybody telling us "It's no big deal," the danger is we might get desensitized and start to believe that, too.

And that would just be kidding ourselves.

"Obscene stories, foolish talk, and coarse jokes—these are not for you," Paul told the Ephesians. "Don't be fooled by those who try to excuse these sins," he warned them (and us), "for the anger of God will fall on all who disobey him. Don't participate in the things these people do" (Ephesians 5:4, 6–7 NLT).

God wants us to keep ourselves pure. He wants us to remember his Spirit lives in us and is constantly working to make us holy, like Jesus. And we can make that happen quicker if we keep the most important part of our bodies—our minds—free from stuff we couldn't share with our moms.

So, how do we get people to stop sending us garbage? Ask them. Send a polite email telling them to please remove your name from their email list for this kind of stuff. If they continue, direct the emails to spam. If it's a BFF doing the sending, something like, "I love you to death, but this is kinda lame. So let's you and I pass on this stuff, okay?" might be a way to handle it.

Most girls, if they're really your friends, will understand. Plus, your reminder may just cause them to take a second look and find that this kind of humor is so not worth damaging your soul for, and may not even be that LOL funny after all.

Food for Thought

Chain letters feed into superstition. Delete 'em—even ones offering blessings. God doesn't bless you because you forwarded an email.

Second Thoughts

This blooper was found in a church bulletin: "The eighth-graders will be presenting Shakespeare's Hamlet in the Church basement Friday at 7:00 p.m. The Congregation is invited to attend this tragedy."

Divine Thoughts

Dearest Jesus, help me to respect you by keeping away from coarse humor.

Your Thoughts:

Devotion 46

"If you keep yourself pure, you will be a special utensil for honorable use. Your life will be clean, and you will be ready for the Master to use you for every good work."

2 Timothy 2:21 NLT

Be Useful . . . Stay Pure

It's your mom's birthday, and you've decided to surprise her by cooking her favorite meal. When you're finished, everything looks and smells awesome. So ... do you put the food in the "good" dishes—the ones that are sparkling clean and ready to be set out? Or do you scrounge up some mismatched, chipped dinnerware that's dusty and needs to be washed?

Right, you want the dinner to be received with joy and enthusiasm. So you serve it in the best possible way: on the good china.

Well, that's what God wants from us. Huh? God wants us to be fancy china? No, but he wants us to be pure and honorable vessels that are cleansed and ready to serve up the Good News of his love, forgiveness, and saving grace.

Paul used this analogy (different kinds of dishes in a house—golden vessels versus earthenware and wooden vessels) in a letter he sent to Timothy. It was meant to remind Timothy to keep away from anything and anyone who would make him unfit to do God's work. Paul also wanted Timothy (and us) to keep in mind that, though Jesus's blood has and will cleanse those who ask forgiveness and profess him as their Savior, it's still up to us to continually strive towards that sanctified state—towards being a perfect vessel like Jesus and for Jesus.

And the way we do that is stay close to him, set ourselves apart for him, and act in a way that will make us worthy to be used by him. "Everyone who confesses the name of the Lord," Paul explained, "must turn away from wickedness" (2 Timothy 2:19). This was especially important for Timothy because as Paul's representative all eyes were on him.

For sure, we all want God to use us to further his kingdom. And if we follow the advice Paul gave Timothy (2 Timothy 2:22), we can—

- Run from anything/anyone that/who will tempt us into improper behavior; and that can include not only impure stuff, but also gossip, displays of anger/rage, jealousy, spitefulness, impatience, and more.
- Follow things that make you want to do right: the Bible, God's Ten Rules, and the Whatever values.
- Pursue faith, love, and peace.
- Enjoy the companionship of those who call on the Lord with pure hearts.

- Lastly, be prepared. We never know when an opportunity will arise to be useful to the Master. And if we keep ourselves pure, we'll be ready.

Food for Thought

The good news is God doesn't only work through saints, Scripture experts, or powerful speakers. He uses girls like you.

Second Thoughts

Is there some fault you have to give up in order to cleanse yourself and be fit to further God's kingdom? Ask him to help you get rid of it.

Divine Thoughts

Jesus, help me stay close to you so I can be useful. Amen.

Your Thoughts:

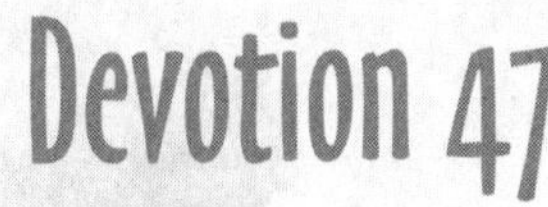

Devotion 47

"And I want women to be modest in their appearance. They should wear decent and appropriate clothing and not draw attention to themselves.... For women who claim to be devoted to God should make themselves attractive by the good things they do."

1 Timothy 2:9–10 NLT

Show and Tell Clothes

Mackenzie came out of the dressing room to show her BFF one of her choices for Estelle's party. "Isn't it way cool?" she said. "I saw it in *Teens & Things Magazine*. It's a little short, but it's half-price. What do you think, Tanya?"

"I think you'd better go with the red one. This one looks like a Band-Aid," Tanya replied. "It's not a little short ...it's *way* short. You'll be pulling it down all night ... that's if your mom even lets you out of the house."

Our clothes can't talk outright, but they can speak volumes about us just the same. They tell our whole story at a glance and can give people either a good or bad impression of the kind of person we are. And it's not just our BFFs who will judge us. It's other girls, guys, parents, teachers, youth ministers, even perfect strangers.

Yup, what we wear can let everyone know whether we're

living for Christ by dressing modestly to get his attention—or living for ourselves by dressing provocatively to get the world's attention.

For sure, many girls do dress to be the center of attraction. They wear tight-fitting clothes, short shorts or low-cut tops, and other "boy magnet" clothes.

And, yeah, they get noticed—but for all the wrong reasons. Believe it, guys aren't riveted on these girls thinking, *Oh, wow, she really looks beautiful,* or *She must be such a nice girl; look how well she dresses.* They're thinking far more improper stuff that may stay with them all day.

So girls who wear revealing clothes are not only hurting themselves, they're also risking damaging others as well. And Jesus warns us about this: "Temptations are inevitable," he says, "but what sorrow awaits the person who does the tempting" (Matthew 18:7 NLT).

The flip side of this is that girls who dress modestly (and look pretty at the same time) can make a statement, too. They can let their clothes tell everyone—loud and clear—that they respect and love God, themselves, and their neighbors enough to forgo the "fashionista" look for a look that shouts "Christianista."

Food for Thought

If Jesus returned suddenly, like, tomorrow, would he find you dressed appropriately?

Second Thoughts

God gave Adam and Eve animal skins to replace their skimpy fig leaves. Read about it in Genesis 3:9-21.

Divine Thoughts

Jesus, help me to remember I should grab attention with what I am inside not what I wear outside. Amen.

Your Thoughts:

Devotion 48

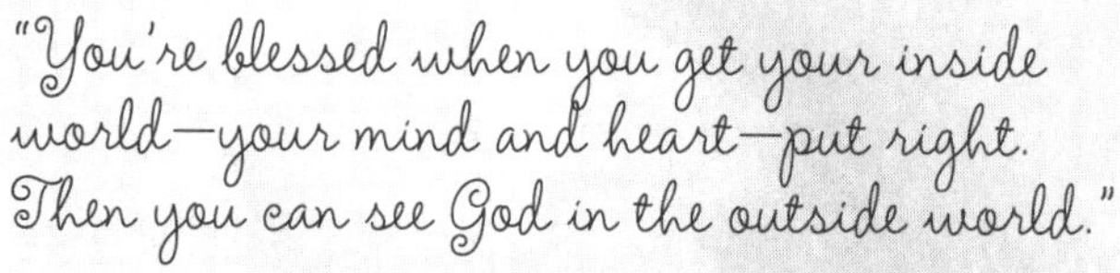

Matthew 5:8 MSG

Like a Child

Want to see God? Duh, *yeah*, who doesn't?

Well, if you keep your heart pure, like that of a little child, you can not only see God when you get to heaven—you can see him right here, right now.

See, very young kids' hearts are squeaky clean and pure—not only because their thoughts are free from the impure stuff the world dishes out—but also because their hearts are still innocent. Kids' hearts are truthful, unprejudiced, and accepting; they're not two-faced or manipulative.

When a child picks a flower, smells it, then hands it to her mom, she does that out of the sheer joy of discovery and love. There are no ulterior motives. It's not because she wants anything back.

"Everything is pure to those whose hearts are pure" (Titus 1:15 NLT), and that describes a small child to a tee.

So although they may be too young to process it, kids see good everywhere—so they see God everywhere. And if we keep our hearts pure, we can, too.

Thing of it is, though, when we're talking "pure," we mean 100 percent pure. "... you cannot live at times one way and at times another way according to how you feel on any given day" (Galatians 5:17 MSG).

Like 100 percent pure silver, our hearts need to be filled with one element only: a pure love that wants to stay close to God, obey him, and live a life that's dedicated to him.

Reading God's Word and obeying its rules, letting the Helper direct our lives, spending time in fellowship with the Lord, praying often, and hanging with girls who love God as much as you do are the best ways to do this.

Still, if you mess up (as we all do) like Jesus's BFF, David, you can pray: "Create in me a pure heart, O God, and renew a steadfast spirit within me" (Psalm 51:10). And God will do just that. If you confess your sins, apologize for disobeying him, and trust in the healing grace of Jesus's cross, God will wash you clean with the blood of his Son. What's more, if you fill your head with thoughts of how much Jesus had to suffer to get and keep you clean, you'll want to do everything you can to stay that way.

Food for Thought

Want to rub elbows with Bible heroes? Jesus promised if we become like little children, we'll be counted among the "greatest in the kingdom of heaven" (Matthew 18:4).

Second Thoughts

Make time to listen to the little ones. Jesus did. You'd be surprised at what you may learn.

Divine Thoughts

Dearest Jesus: help me to keep my thoughts pure, so I can see you everywhere. Amen.

Your Thoughts:

"Don't be drunk with wine, because that will ruin your life. Instead be filled with the Holy Spirit."

Ephesians 5:18 NLT

Alcohol: It's Not a Problem Solver

Renee was acting goofy when she arrived at the football stadium.

"What's up?" her friend Haley asked. "You okay?"

"Fine," Renee said, grinning. "I knew Ritchie would be here, and, like, I really want to talk to him. But I get tongue-tied around boys. So I brought a little 'courage.'" With that, Renee opened her bag to reveal a small water bottle that *wasn't* filled with water. "From dad's bar," she whispered, giggling. A little while later, Renee felt nauseous and had to get a ride home. She never *did* get to talk to Ritchie.

Alcohol in and of itself isn't a bad thing. In fact, wine is the symbol of the new covenant, and we see it featured prominently in Jesus's first miracle. It's only when, like anything else, we misuse it that problems arise. Renee thought that drinking would relax her and take away her fears about meeting a boy she liked. So she forgot about God, acted deceitfully, and wound up hurting herself in the bargain.

A way better plan would have been for her to talk to God, lean on his Holy Spirit, and allow the Helper to quiet her nervousness, be with her, and direct her path. Knowing the Spirit was in her corner and trusting he would strengthen her and calm her jitters would surely have been more of a bolster than a swig of vodka. Then, too, if she had trusted the Helper and taken a pro-active stand, he probably could have led her to some other confidence-building idea, like asking her BFF to rehearse what she would say to Ritchie beforehand. Instead she relied on alcohol, which only left her sick and embarrassed.

Some kids think drinking is the answer to insecurities. So they nip liquor from their parents, or hang with kids who have access to beer and malt drinks. Then they talk too much, act silly, or do things (risky or improper) they would never do otherwise.

And when the buzz wears off, they are left just as insecure. Only on top of that, they feel empty and ashamed. Proverbs hits the nail on the head when it comes to excessive alcohol: "Wine and beer make people loud and uncontrolled; it is not wise to get drunk on them" (Proverbs 20:1 NCV).

Especially when there is a gentle, loving Spirit who is ready to help us deal with our fears and insecurities if we will only ask him and trust him.

Food for Thought

What Bible character complained of not being good with words? Find out in Exodus 4:10-17.

Second Thoughts

God wants us to obey those in authority (1 Peter 2:13). Under-age drinkers are not only disappointing God, they're also not obeying the law.

Divine Thoughts

Jesus, teach me to rely on your Holy Spirit when I feel nervous, shy, or insecure. Amen.

Your Thoughts:

Devotion 50

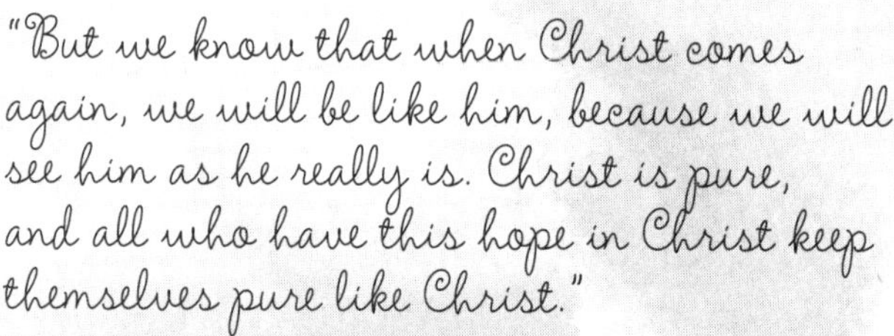

1 John 3:2–3 NCV

Pure and Simple

"Did you see what ChattyGirl posted today?" Alli asked Megan.

"Not yet," Megan answered.

"Well, you know Anonymous asked for advice about staying pure last week," Alli said. "So ChattyGirl replied today with this: she said that if someone wants to involve us in improper stuff by saying that everybody reads, listens to, or does impure things—that it's up to us to remind them we're not trying to be like everybody. We're trying to be like Jesus."

"She got 67 'likes.' She's my new hero."

ChattyGirl is Jesus's new hero as well. That's because he knows how important remaining pure is to our spiritual and bodily well-being. It shows we respect him, our parents, our husband-to-be, and ourselves. What's more, making a commitment when we're young to stay pure closes the door to worry, fear, and other problems and keeps our minds focused on what's important: building a solid faith based on learning about Jesus, who we are in him, and what direction his plans are taking us.

See, our primary mission in life is to get to know Jesus and to become more like him. And the best part of that challenge is that the more we get to know him, the more we want to become like him.

Now, we know that Jesus is good, kind, and loving. We know he is smart, that he had patience, and is humble. We know he is generous and caring. And Scripture also tells us he was pure. (1 John 3:3 TLB)

Though he is God, he was also man and had a human body with senses just like ours. And though there certainly must have been a lot of immoral stuff going on around him, Jesus didn't let it affect him. He closed his mind and heart to it. In everything he did, he used his body to give glory to his Father.

So it makes sense that if we want to become like Jesus, our challenge is to stay pure as well. And as we all know by now, the key to keeping our bodies in check is to keep our minds in check. (Remember SLAM, LAMB and SCRAM in Devotion # 3).

The world we live in is filled with immorality—that's an unfortunate fact. But the Bible says our bodies (and our minds) were not made for immorality. "They were made for the Lord" (1 Corinthians 6:13 NLT). And if we keep our thoughts on Whatever (is true, right, pure, noble, praiseworthy, lovely, admirable, and excellent), we can make sure we are worthy of him.

Food for Thought

Acting impulsively, without thinking, can blow up in our faces. Esau acted impulsively, gave away something precious to satisfy his immediate hunger, and regretted it. Read about him in Genesis 25:27-34.

Second Thoughts

It's not easy to "take captive every thought to make it obedient to Christ" (2 Corinthians 10:5). But with the grace of the Helper and a dedicated effort on our part, we can.

Divine Thoughts

Dearest Jesus, help me to seek out people, places, and things that honor you, so I can stay pure and be like you. Amen.

Your Thoughts:

Section 6

Whatever's Lovely

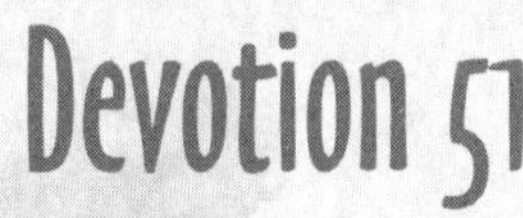

Devotion 51

"Three things will last forever—faith, hope, and love—and the greatest of these is love."

1 Corinthians 13:13 NLT

Real Love—It's Lovely

Something that's lovely, the dictionary tells us, "elicits love." So when we think about what's lovely, it's kind of natural to also think about love.

But the kind of love the world is pedaling is more like a fun-house mirror—full of distortions—than what the Bible tells us to go after, "as if your life depended on it" (1 Corinthians 14:1 MSG).

See, according to what the world (and a lot of ads) would have us believe, love equals sex appeal. And the amount of love we can expect depends on how attractive we are to the opposite sex.

What's more, how attractive we are depends on which products we use and what "stuff" we buy—perfumes, like "Irresistible," or shoes with heels that are like a clown's stilts.

The world also suggests not only the ways we can get people to love us, but also the ways we can show our love to them. And that's by giving them pricey material stuff—because society measures how much we love someone by how much money we're willing to spend on them.

Thankfully, we have more than the world's impression of love to go by. And if we "Follow the way of love" the Bible gives us (1 Corinthians 14:1), we'll find it has nothing to do with sex appeal or "stuff," and everything to do with God and the Bible. Following that way will lead us to love itself, because that's what Jesus is—the greatest expression of love ever. "The greatest love a person can show is to die for his friends" (John 15:13 NCV).

Jesus's BFF, Paul, said this love—the kind that comes from Jesus and IS Jesus—is a way of life and a gift that will outlast truth and hope. Paul said if we do all kinds of good things, but don't have it, we're nothing (1 Corinthians 13:1-3). He also explained how this kind of love acts:

- It doesn't give up; cares more for others than for self.
- It doesn't strut; doesn't have a swelled head.
- It doesn't force itself on others; isn't always "Me first."
- It doesn't fly off the handle; doesn't keep score of the sins of others.

This kind of love trusts God, "Always, always looks for

the best, never looks back, but keeps going to the end (1 Corinthians 13:7 MSG).

Now, *that's* totally out-of-this-world lovely love. You think?

Food for Thought

The words of 1 Corinthians 13 are often recited at weddings. Can you guess why?

Second Thoughts

Some girls try things like shopping, eating, or over-achieving when they don't feel loved. What they should try is Jesus instead.

Divine Thoughts

Dearest Jesus, help me to love you as much as you love me. Amen.

Your Thoughts:

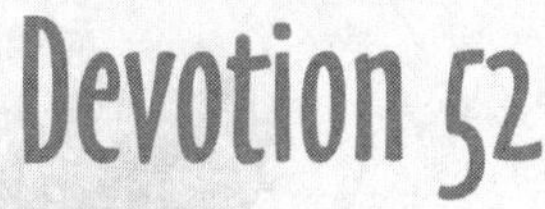

Devotion 52

"Some people make cutting remarks, but the words of the wise bring healing."

Proverbs 12:18 NLT

The Rose and the Thorn

Think quick: What's lovelier, a thorn or a rose?

No brainer. Rose wins. Roses are lovely to look at. They're soft and smell good. They make you feel good just to have around. If you could have a million, that wouldn't be a bad thing. If you got even a single one from a secret admirer, you'd be floating on air.

A thorn, on the other hand, well, it's ugly and prickly. If you received a vase full of just stems with thorns, you'd probably throw them out.

Okay, here's the point: God wants us to be like a rose in someone's day, not like a thorn. "Love one another with genuine affection," the Bible says, "and take delight in honoring one another" (Romans 12:10 NLT). One way to do that is to get rid of sarcasm.

You know what that is—saying what you don't mean, and

meaning things you don't flat out say. It's zapping people with insults, put-downs, and disrespectful answers.

"Yeah, right. Thanks a lot," Vicky says to her parents when she means just the opposite.

"Go to the mall? I'd love to," Dawn says to a friend she's angry with. "How's never? Is never good for you?"

"Hey, Debby, speak up," Pam says to a girl on her cell. "They can't hear you in Antarctica." And that's mild by comparison. Some girls say horrible things—insults and back-stabbing barbs they would never have the nerve to say outright. They get the crowd's attention. They make people crack up. Then, they hide behind "just kidding," and expect the person on the receiving end of this "joke" to just "forget about it." If they don't, that person, for sure, is labeled a poor sport with no sense of humor.

These girls think they're cool. They think they're clever. They think they're hysterical.

But God doesn't. Because using hurtful sarcasm isn't funny in his book. His book tells us to love not hurt. His book tells us to encourage people and be kind to them.

His book says, "Do not let any unwholesome talk come out of your mouths, but only what is helpful for building others up according to their needs, that it may benefit those who listen" (Ephesians 4:29).

At the start of every day, it's up to you to decide: *Will I be a rose or a thorn today?*

Food For Thought

When someone's being sarcastic, resist the urge to return the taunt. Say, "Hey, if there's something bugging you, let's talk about it."

Second Thoughts

Can't stand girls with thorny tongues? Yes you can—because your souls have been cleansed from selfishness and hatred when you trusted Christ to save you ... (1 Peter 1:22).

Divine Thoughts

Sweet Jesus, you returned love for insults. Help me to do the same. Amen.

Your Thoughts:

Devotion 53

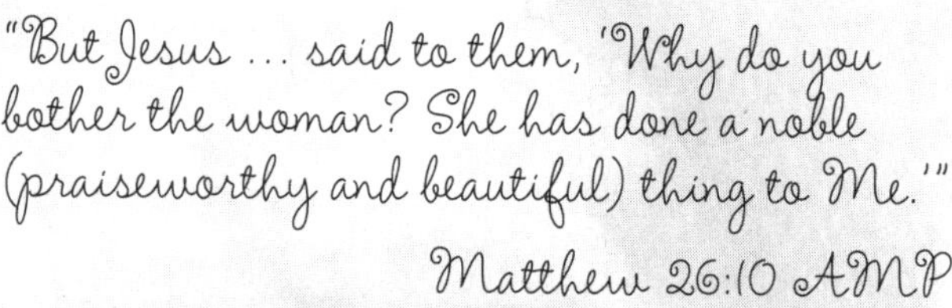

"But Jesus ... said to them, 'Why do you bother the woman? She has done a noble (praiseworthy and beautiful) thing to Me.'"

Matthew 26:10 AMP

The Woman with the Perfume

There's an awesome story in all four Gospels that illustrates how far one woman would go to show her love, reverence, and gratitude to Jesus.

Here's the scene: A woman walks into a house where Jesus was a guest, breaks open an expensive jar of perfume, and pours it on Jesus's head and feet, crying as she does. Then she kisses his feet and dries the tears and perfume with her hair.

Now, everyone (but Jesus) found this shocking, brazen, and wasteful. But if we look closer, we can see it was driven by what's true, noble, right, pure, lovely, admirable, excellent, and praiseworthy.

Okay, the gesture seemed bizarre to others because they didn't realize—or refused to believe—the **truth** about Jesus—that he was the Messiah, the Savior. But the woman knew and believed. She was one of the few who "got" who Jesus is and what he was about to do.

Now, her background might have been questionable. But she did an **admirable** and **noble** deed. She risked contempt and withstood verbal abuse to anoint Jesus as her Savior. Jesus also said her anointing him was preparing his body for burial (Matthew 26:12).

And when Jesus's host appeared to diss him by not offering the water, oil, and kiss due a visitor—the woman did the **right** thing. She gave Jesus what the host ignored—in a most humble and respectful way.

But the guests were stunned. Women back then didn't touch men in public. So, to kiss and dry Jesus's feet with her hair, to them, was shameful. Still, the woman acted with **pure** intentions, out of **pure** affection.

For sure, the onlookers thought what the woman did was wasteful—that the perfume should have been sold to help the poor. What Jesus saw, though, was a **lovely** gesture. He said the woman had done a "beautiful" and "**praiseworthy**" thing. He even told the others to quit giving her "a hard time" (Matthew 26:10 MSG).

Why such a lavish gift? Why not? Jesus deserves the best. So the woman gave him the most **excellent** thing she owned. And when she poured the perfume on Jesus, mixing it with her tears, she gave him something else that was **excellent:** her love.

How about us? Like the woman with the perfume, can we pour out our over-the-top love on Jesus ... like he did for us on the cross? Let's try.

Food for Thought

When girls drink, smoke, and wear heavy makeup and perfume, you can smell it on them. Would you call that "lovely?"

Second Thoughts

Bible experts differ about who the "woman" was. But that isn't as important as what she did. Read all four versions, Matthew 26:6-13, Mark 14:1-9, Luke 7:36-50, and John 12:1-8.

Divine Thoughts

Jesus, help me to never avoid showing you my love because of what others may think. Amen.

Your Thoughts:

Devotion 54

"...he is altogether lovely!"

Song of Songs 5:16

Way Lovely

The word "lovely" sounds a bit old-fashioned—something our moms or grandmas would use to describe a dress, scenery, or even a baby. It's not a word *we* tend to use a lot.

But the Bible is full of references to things that are lovely: God's Temple, timely advice, the daughters of Job (Psalm 84:1; Proverbs 25:11; Job 42:15). And in those instances, the word has a lot more clout. It means way fabulous, the best, awesome, the ultimate. For example, the Song of Songs has been read as an analogy of Jesus as the bridegroom and the church as the bride, and describes the bride as calling her intended (Jesus), "altogether lovely" (Song of Songs 5:15).

Technically the word means loveable, and inspiring or eliciting love and that, for sure, describes Jesus. Fact is he is lovely in every sense of the word for a gazillion million reasons. Let's look at a few:

- He's the source. Jesus is loveliness. And if anything is lovely, it is because of him. Nothing we can want or have is lovelier than he is.

- His character is altogether lovely. He is kind, gentle, strong, patient, sympathetic, merciful, forgiving, humble, and of course, truthful, noble, pure, admirable, praiseworthy, and totally excellent.

- His actions are altogether lovely. He wants only the best for us. He loves us, redeemed us, and protects us.

- His friendship is altogether lovely. He listens to us and comforts us. He'll never forsake or leave us.

- His sacrifice was altogether lovely. Jesus was his loveliest on the cross—even battered and bloody—because it was there that he poured out all his love for us. And with that ...

- He made us lovely to God. Because Jesus died and washed away all of our sins, he got rid of all the ugliness so we'd be acceptable to God.

- His resurrection was altogether lovely because it conquered death and sin and gave us life.

Right now, we only have a hazy glimpse of Jesus's loveliness. But if we believe in him, keeping his commandments and following his Word, we'll be able to see him in person one day. And just think, like the bride in the Song of Songs, we'll be able to say, "Jesus, you are 'altogether lovely'" (Song of Songs 5:16).

Food for Thought

Remember that you are lovely in God's eyes. So don't get so wrapped up in how your hair or your clothes look.

Second Thoughts

Do something nice for your mom or your dad. But don't tell them you did it. See how lovely it makes their day.

Divine Thoughts

Dearest Jesus, help me to act in way that lets others see how lovely you are. Amen.

Your Thoughts:

Devotion 55

"Let your gentleness be evident to all. The Lord is near."

Philippians 4:5

A Little Gentleness

Catalina saw Melinda pick up the brand-new edition of *Teen Beauty* at the hairdresser's, look around, then stash it in her bag.

Later, Catalina cornered Melinda. "I saw you nip that magazine, kiddo," she said. "I'm no angel, but I know that's stealing. Perhaps you had better take yourself back and return it, you think?"

Melinda—cheeks burning—got up into Cat's face: "Yeah, and perhaps you'd better mind your own stupid business, you think?"

Whoa! That went well ... NOT!

Yeah, but Catalina probably should have known better. Nobody likes to be clobbered over the head with their wrongdoing. Yes, we're supposed to say something when our BFF steps out of line. But there's a gentler, more loving, Christ-like way to get messages across—a way that'll keep peace and net us better results.

The Bible says we should "be patient with difficult people," so that they "will come to their senses and escape from the devil's trap" (2 Timothy 2:24, 26 NLT). Because that's what we're really trying to do: get our BFF's attention in a calm, caring way so she'll have a change of heart, turn away from wrongdoing, and turn back to Christ. That's, like, totally not going to happen if we're finger-pointing and bossy. So we have to choose our words and our tone super carefully.

See, we all get uptight when we do something wrong. We feel guilty and vulnerable. Since we already realize we're off base, if someone gives us a gentle nudge—that might just be the voice of sweet reasonableness we need to get back on track.

The Bible says God sent Jesus to save the world, not to condemn it (John 3:17). That's why he spent lots of time with sinners—so he could tell the people who needed it most about God's love and forgiveness. And he, of all people, had the power and the right to bawl them out. But Jesus condemned the sin, not the sinner. He told the adulterous woman after the people who accused her left, "I also don't judge you guilty. You may go now, but don't sin anymore" (John 8:11 NCV). So, let's give gentle reminders to our friends, all the while thinking how we'd feel in their place. Let's be like Jesus, "gentle and humble in heart" (Matthew 11:29).

Food for Thought

Jesus left us the Helper, his Spirit, to live in our hearts and help us grow in gentleness and kindness when we practice love.

Second Thoughts

You've just messed up. Think about the way you would like a BFF to remind you, and act the same when it's *you* doing the reminding.

Divine Thoughts

Dearest Jesus, in a world full of things that are rough and violent, let me show I belong to you by being lovely, gentle, and kind. Amen.

Your Thoughts:

Devotion 56

"Let's march into his presence singing praises,
lifting the rafters with our hymns!
And why? Because God is the best,
High King over all the gods."

Psalm 95:2–3 MSG

A Joyful Noise

Johanna went to her gran's new house for Easter. She had never been to the local church and didn't know what to expect.

The service was lively and filled with music. The youth choir, backed by two killer guitars, a piano, and drum, led the congregation in some classic and some modern hymns. People young and old, including granny, were totally into it. Johanna, who always thought her voice was lame, finally joined in, too. When she left the church, she felt a sense of joy she couldn't quite explain.

The Bible says, "Shout for joy to the Lord, all the earth. Worship the Lord with gladness; come before him with joyful songs." (Psalm 100:1-2).

It doesn't say those with voices like Taylor Swift sing to the Lord; all others forget about it. It doesn't say sing to the

Lord but don't sing too loud; otherwise, people sitting next to you will think you're way weird. Nope. It says "Worship the LORD with gladness," and that means enthusiasm.

See, music is an important part of our worship. And if we don't enter into it fully, we're not giving God our best. We're missing out on our chance to "Tell the world how glorious he is" (Psalm 66:2 NLT). We're letting other people's reactions or our own insecurities hold us back.

God's buddy David never had that problem. He was a free-spirited, over-the-top worshiper. When he and his men brought the Ark of the Covenant back to Jerusalem, David threw off his kingly robe, and wearing just a short tunic, sang, leapt, and danced in the streets praising God.

He didn't care what people thought of him. He didn't care who was watching. He was focused on God. And when his wife Michal saw him singing and worshipping in the street that way, she said he acted like a fool. But that didn't faze David. "I was before the Lord," David told her (2 Samuel 6:21).

See, all David's life, God had done some pretty cool stuff for him. And this total, all-out, body-and-soul worship was David's bold way of expressing his thanks and joy.

God has done some pretty neat things for us as well, and along with everything else that sings his praises—the birds, trees, mountains, and hills—we should, too. Whether our voice is sweet as a songbird or more like a squeaky mouse, the Lord hears it all. And to his ears, there's nothing lovelier.

Food for Thought

Music can uplift or degrade. Give your downloads the Whatever test. If song lyrics don't pass, take a pass.

Second Thoughts

If Justin Bieber came to your church, would you be too embarrassed to sing, clap, and join in? So why should singing for Jesus be any different?

Divine Thoughts

Mighty Lord, remind me I'm not in a singing contest at church. I'm there to give you praise and celebrate that you're the greatest! Amen.

Your Thoughts:

Devotion 57

"... whatever is lovely ... think about such things."

Philippians 4:8

Think Lovely

Rita looked at the kittens, a jumble of tiny, whiskered fur balls snuggled close to their mama. *They are, like, so beautiful,* she thought.

She kept that lovely image in her head all day at school. Thinking of the momma cat and her kittens made Rita feel calm and happy. It also led her to thoughts of God—how awesome and lovely he must be, and how much fun he must have had creating all the animals. As she walked to her locker, she just had to smile.

When we look at something lovely, we get a glimpse of the magnificence of God—who is love, and who made and sustains everything *with* love. The Bible says we can see "God's invisible qualities" and "divine nature" in what he has made (Romans 1:20). So it's no surprise we're drawn to lovely things and that those things lead us to thoughts of gratitude and praise for the Creator.

The flip side is because sin has entered the world, many things that *can* be lovely—movies, books, music, websites, TV shows—are anything but. They've been spoiled. But, the world still insists these violent and impure things are just entertainment. Graphic murder scene? It's only acting. Questionable song lyrics? No problem. In one ear, out the other.

But that's not the way our minds work. The Bible asks us, "Can anyone walk on red-hot coals without burning his feet?" (Proverbs 6:28 GWT). Don't think so. Same thing applies here. If we see, listen to, or read gross, stupid, dark, dirty, gory stuff, it's going to affect us. We'll wind up with a head full of disturbing thoughts—thoughts that are as far removed from God, his love, and his magnificence as light is from darkness.

The Holy Spirit can help us steer clear of this stuff, though, if we ask him. With his power and strength working through and in us, we can close our eyes and minds to the loveless and degrading, and fill our thoughts and hearts with the lovely and uplifting. The Bible says the Spirit can help us want the good and hate the wrong and that if the Spirit controls our minds, we'll have "life and peace" (Romans 8:6).

Oh, boy, now, isn't *that* a lovely thought?

Food for Thought

Can people see the Lord's loveliness reflected in you?

Second Thoughts

List ten lovely things you saw, heard, or read this week like a wedding, a summer garden, or an orange-lollipop sunset. Sit and think about how they reflect God's love.

Divine Thoughts

Dear Holy Spirit, there are so many lovely, God-inspired things I can think about. Help me to. Amen.

Your Thoughts:

Devotion 58

"O Israel, can I not do to you as this potter has done to his clay?"

Jeremiah 18:6 NLT

How God Molds Us

Marina was caught passing off an essay she bought on the Internet as her own. She admitted she was wrong, apologized, and took her punishment.

"What a dummy I've been," she said later to her BFF. "I've let everybody down. God must be so disappointed in me. He must think I'm a real loser."

We all do things we shouldn't now and again. And it's times like these when the lesson of the potter and the clay from Jeremiah 18 can comfort, renew, and give us hope in God's forgiveness and grace. Let's see how the story applies.

Okay, so the Israelites were sinning left, right, and center. And God wanted them to know he'd have to punish them if they didn't repent. But he also wanted them to understand that if they did repent, he would restore and bless them. So he told his messenger Jeremiah to give them that news.

But first, God sent Jeremiah to a local potter. When he arrived, the potter had what looked like a jar on the wheel. But the shape wasn't coming out right. So the potter squashed the clay back into a lump and began again.

God wanted Jeremiah to see this because it demonstrated a point. "As the clay is in the potter's hand," God told Jeremiah, "so are you in my hand" (Jeremiah 18:6 NLT).

With this visual and that single sentence, God was showing *and* telling Jeremiah things he wanted the people (and us) to understand about our relationship with him:

God is the Master Potter; we are the lumpy clay. Because of our sins, we may have to be reworked and reshaped to get rid of our imperfections. God may have to add more water (grace from his Holy Spirit) to make us pliable. And he may just have to squish us down and start over. This may hurt. We may have to go through hard times. But we'll always be in the careful, loving hands of the Potter. So we shouldn't resist or worry.

What's more, God the Master Potter will never toss defective clay (us) away. He'll continue working with it (us) until it is molded into something useful to him.

That's why we should never give up when we mess up. Instead, let's keep in mind that the Master Potter is always ready to remake our lumpy selves into something lovely—something he has wanted us to resemble from the beginning of time—the most precious of all vessels: Jesus.

Food for Thought

God reshaped and reworked Paul—who went from enemy of Jesus to his BFF and from persecuting the church to establishing it. Read more in Acts 9:1-28.

Second Thoughts

A potter has to be way gentle, yet firm, when he is creating. He also must have extraordinary patience and dedication. A lovely image of God, for sure.

Divine Thoughts

Dearest God, thank you so much for never giving up on me. Amen.

Your Thoughts:

Devotion 59

"I am the light of the world. Whoever follows me will never walk in darkness, but will have the light of life."

John 8:12

Walking in the Son-Light

Jenny and her friend Pauline went to the lake to take photos for camera club.

"Look how the light shines through those trees," Jenny said. "Wow, what a shot! Yikes, and the water's like diamonds."

"Yeah, it was too cloudy last time," Pauline said. "The sun makes all the difference."

The sun has a way of making things lovelier, brighter, more in focus—and so does the Son. The Bible says, "God is light; in him there is no darkness at all" (1 John 1:5). So when we walk with Jesus, everything is different. And if we obey his commandments and study his Word, he can help us avoid much of the bleakness we see around us.

Nobody likes to walk in darkness. We can't see where we're going; we may trip and fall. It's, like, way scary, too. There could be strangers who want to hurt us. And who'd want to hang out in the dark anyway?

Believe it or not, there are people who do. "All who do evil hate the light and refuse to go near it for fear their sins will be exposed" (John 3:20 NLT). Well, that's not for us. We *want* the Light. And Jesus offers us His light—the light of life which—

- Lets us see; no more stumbling in the dark (Psalm 119:165 MSG)
- Points us in the right direction (John 12:35)
- Exposes evil things (Ephesians 5:14 NLT) so we can't be fooled
- Helps us have fellowship with others, and cleanses us from sin and guilt (1 John 1:7)
- Reveals pockets of darkness (sins) in our own lives so we can admit them, ask forgiveness, and change (1 John 1:9)
- Finally, it attracts others. And that's where we figure in most.

See, when we walk with Jesus, his light is so powerful, it shines through us. Others see it and witness how the light affects our lives. They see us spreading love, not hate; helping out, not dropping out; building others up, not tearing them down—and our example makes them want to walk with us. In this way, Jesus uses *us* as a living testimony to get people to leave the darkness.

And once they come to know, as we do, how lovely it feels to walk in the Son-light, it really *will* make all the difference.

Food for Thought

Want to be a show-off for Jesus? You can if you "let your light shine before others, that they may see your good deeds and glorify your Father in heaven" (Matthew 5:16).

Second Thoughts

If someone asks you a faith question, but you don't know the answer, tell them you'll find out and get back to them. That's shining your light.

Divine Thoughts

Dearest Jesus, help me to act in a way that will make more girls want to walk with you. Amen.

Your Thoughts:

Section 7

Whatever's Admirable

Devotion 60

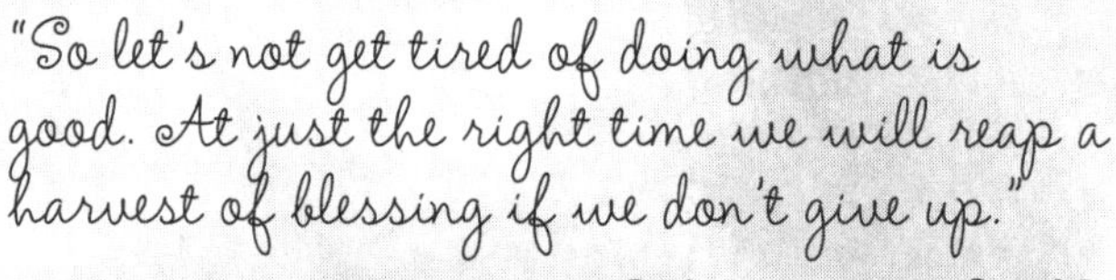

Galatians 6:9 NLT

Hanging in There

Natasha and Janice had signed up to be vacation Bible school volunteers. But half-way through the session, the newness wore off, and Janice decided it was way too much work. Besides, she had volunteered for a week, and that was enough. So she told the VBS director she was burnt out. Then she quit.

Natasha hung in for the entire three weeks, honoring her commitment, and when VBS ended, she felt a sense of real accomplishment. What's more, on the last day, the class thanked her with a hand-painted card.

Because of her commitment, Natasha not only scored points with her students, she also scored points with God. The Bible says those who don't tire of doing good can count themselves as faithful servants, receive a heavenly reward, and learn to become more like Jesus, who always "went around doing good" (Acts 10:38 NLT).

See, doing good isn't only admirable—it's one of our jobs as Christians. God wants us to be his helpers. He wants to accomplish his will through us. He wants to be able to say, like the master in Jesus's parable, "Well done, my good and faithful servant" (Matthew 25:21 NLT). But to do that, we have to stay the course—continue doing good—not for a day or even a year but until God's work is completed. And that won't be until Jesus comes again.

When he does, girls who've remained faithful because of the "strength and energy that God supplies" (1 Peter 4:11 NLT) will get paid in full. They'll receive their inheritance; they'll get their prize; and they'll be with Jesus for eternity. Awesome!

Okay, and if we flub it?

That's when we ...

Recharge: Consistent, long periods of ministering can take its toll. That's when we take a break, rest, revive ourselves—then continue with our good works. Even Jesus did that.

Reconnect: Plug into our Power Source by praying, reading Scripture, and asking God to "Be our strength every morning" (Isaiah 33:2).

Remember: Remind ourselves that doing good is a privilege that helps us become more like the Lord.

If we think of it, if anyone had the right to be weary it was Jesus. His "doing good works" schedule was off the charts.

Everywhere he went, crowds flocked to him clamoring, "Heal us, teach us, feed us." Yet he never threw in the towel.

Nope, Jesus wasn't a quitter. He continued until he did all that was expected of him—until, on the cross, at the very end he could say, "It is finished" (John 19:30).

So let's honor our commitments to do good and "be strong and steady, always enthusiastic about the Lord's work" (1 Corinthians 15:58 NLT).

Food for Thought

Did you know God "will not grow tired or weary" (Isaiah 40:28), and his "power is made perfect" when we're weak? (2 Corinthians 12:9).

Second Thoughts

Read how God pumped Elijah up when he wanted to give up in 1 Kings 19:1-18.

Divine Thoughts

Jesus, when I get tired or bored of doing good, remind me to look to you for strength. Amen.

Your Thoughts:

Devotion 61

"Then a poor widow came and dropped in two small coins."

Mark 12:42 NLT

Giving from the Heart

Sometimes it's the small things that make us admirable in the eyes of God—like giving the best from the goodness of our hearts.

When her church was having a clothes drive for earthquake victims, Ginger, a girl from a poor family, did just that. Her things were mostly hand-me-downs. But she did have a really neat pair of jeans she'd bought with babysitting money. She hadn't worn them yet. But then she figured, *those girls lost everything, and I'm blessed to have so much.* So she did the admirable thing: She gave her special jeans to the drive, quietly. Nobody even noticed.

Nobody, that is, except Jesus. See, Jesus doesn't care so much about what we give, or how much. What impresses him most is a girl who gives without holding back out of love for her neighbor—a girl who gives without complaining or expecting anything in return—a girl who doesn't make a big show so everyone sees.

That's why Jesus was so taken with the poor widow. He noticed her right away. Little wonder, since next to the rich Temple-goers, dudes who were puffed up and pleased with themselves, she stood out like a sore thumb. These guys made sure everyone saw them as they put gobs of money they didn't need into the treasury box.

The widow, on the other hand, put her coins in humbly—the right way to make an offering to God. And she didn't skimp. She had two small coins, and rather than keep one for herself, she dropped both in. This truly was a sacrifice because she didn't know where her next meal would come from. Still, the widow must have believed (from past experience?) God would take care of her. So she gave her best—everything she had.

Jesus was so moved, he called his disciples over to show them what she had done. She gave "all she had to live on," he said (Mark 12:44).

The Bible says we should be generous to those in need, always being ready to share with others." When we do this, we'll be storing up real treasure for ourselves in heaven (1 Timothy 6:18–19 NLT).

So next time you give something, give your best, like the widow, in the spirit of love straight from your heart. Then leave the door open, and let God's blessings flow back atcha.

Food for Thought

The widow wasn't embarrassed to give such a small gift. She gave it cheerfully, not concerned with what others thought.

Second Thoughts

The Bible says when you give gifts, do it in private, because "Then your Father, who sees what is done in secret, will reward you" (Matthew 6:4).

Divine Thoughts

Dearest Jesus, sometimes I want to keep the best for myself. Remind me sharing is what you want me to do. Amen.

Your Thoughts:

Devotion 62

"Caleb interrupted, called for silence before Moses, and said, 'Let's go up and take the land—now. We can do it.'"

Numbers 13:30 MSG

Be a Possibilitarian

The Making a Difference club recommendations were due to the director on Friday. But when LeeAnne suggested helping with the inner city reading program, everyone shot her down.

"Look," April said, "that kind of a project takes a lot of time and effort. And we're not trained, for Pete's sake. It's a bad idea, LeeAnne."

"Yeah," said Tamara. "They'll come once, then blow us off. Let's just have a can collection, like we always do. We can handle that, no sweat."

But LeeAnne wouldn't let it go. She knew she'd get flack. Still, she had to insist: "Guys, this is our ministry. And we've dedicated our work to Jesus, so he'll help us. We can *really* make a difference teaching kids to read. I'm going to suggest it."

Sometimes, we just have to take a stand. We have to become a Possibilitarian. We have to speak up, go against peer pressure, and ignore the naysayers who tell us "It can't be done," or "Let's do something easier." That's the kind of attitude God admires and blesses.

Both Joshua and his friend Caleb had that mindset. When Moses sent them and ten others to check out Canaan, these two were the only ones who returned with a good report. Everyone else said, "The men are like giants; we'll get slaughtered. We're not going" (Numbers 13:28–33).

Even after Caleb reminded the people that the inhabitants of Canaan "have no protection, but the Lord is with us!" (Numbers 14:9 NLT), the crowd still refused to believe. Talk about short memories. They forgot the God who saved them from the fierce Egyptians. They forgot the God who provided food and water in the desert. They forgot the God who made a covenant that they'd get this land.

Not surprisingly, God got angry. He banned everyone but Caleb and Joshua from Canaan and sent the unbelievers back to wander in the desert.

Okay, so why was Caleb able to see the possibilities where others saw defeat, doom, and gloom? The Bible says he "followed the LORD my God wholeheartedly" (Joshua 14:9). He thought: *We might not be able to take those dudes, but for sure, God can. God said this land is ours and I believe him.*

Yup, sometimes we just have to stand our ground. We have to pray, ask the Helper for courage, and as Caleb said, have faith that with God's help, "we can certainly do" (Numbers 13:30) whatever it is we feel God is calling us to do. Remember the naysayers never made it to the Promised Land ... but Caleb and Joshua did.

Food for Thought

Jericho's "giants" were more afraid of the Israelites than the Israelites were of them. Read more in Joshua 2:9-11 TLB.

Second Thoughts

Have you ever spoken your mind when everyone else thought differently? How did that make you feel?

Divine Thoughts

Dearest Jesus, even if it means going against the crowd, I want to be a Possibilitarian for you. Amen.

Your Thoughts:

Devotion 63

"'Yes it is, Lord,' she said, 'Even the dogs eat the crumbs that fall from their master's table.' Then Jesus said to her, 'Woman, you have great faith! Your request is granted.'"

Matthew 15:27–28

True Grit

"You're too young to volunteer," the manager at the local pet shelter said. But that didn't keep Olivia from coming in regularly to apply.

Three months later, the manager gave in. "Okay, Miss-Determined-to-Work-Here," she said. "Come with me, and I'll show you what to do."

Girls who give up if they don't get what they want right away can't expect a lot of success in anything, really. On the other hand, everyone admires a girl with persistence, especially God.

Persistence, the Merriam-Webster's dictionary says, is a "quality that allows you to continue doing something or trying to do something even though it's difficult." A girl who's persistent doesn't lose heart even when she can't feel God's presence, even when it seems as though he doesn't care, even when she feels he's not answering her prayers. When it seems like there's no hope, that's when she keeps on praying and never quits.

Jesus met a woman like that. She was a bold, Canaanite mother with four strikes against her: she was a pagan, a non-Jew, a woman alone pestering a group of male strangers (and not in her inside voice, for sure), and had a demon-possessed daughter whom she insisted Jesus heal.

His answer? "Jesus did not answer a word" (Matthew 15:23). It was as though he wanted more from this woman and knew his silence would bring it out. And when he did speak and seemed to say "No," she didn't walk away angry or get depressed. She did the opposite: "She came and, kneeling, worshipped Him and kept praying, Lord, help me!" (Matthew 15:25 AMP).

Even when Jesus hinted she was like a dog trying to snatch bread meant for children, like a dog she held on, accepting Jesus on *his* terms. Even a crumb, she said, would be enough. And with that, Jesus healed her daughter.

What about us? Are we willing to be that persistent? To keep praying and knocking on God's door, boldly asking him for patience to wait for his answers, help when we need to resist temptation, strength to praise him when things get rough, and grace to thank him for proving us worthy through problems?

If we are, then like the Canaanite woman, our Lord will surely take care of our needs. BTW, Jesus doesn't mind if we pester him; in fact, he kind of likes it.

Food for Thought

Jesus may just have been trying to teach his disciples a thing or two about not losing heart though the Canaanite woman. You think?

Second Thoughts

Jesus told a story about another persistent woman. Read about her in Luke 18:1-8.

Divine Thoughts

Jesus, sometimes when I pray and the answer doesn't come quickly enough, I lose heart. Help me to trust You and keep praying. Amen.

Your Thoughts:

Devotion 64

*"Fire goes out without wood,
and quarrels disappear when gossip
stops."*

Proverbs 26:20 NLT

Whatever . . . Stops Gossip

Ever play telephone? The game where a girl whispers something to another girl, and on down the line until the last girl repeats what the first girl is *supposed* to have said, and it's so different, everybody cracks up?

Gossip's like that. But instead of ROTFLOL funny, what's passed along can destroy reputations, friendships, and self-esteem, for both the target of the gossip and the person telling the tales.

It seems harmless, getting together with close friends and having an innocent gab fest. Yet it all depends on the subject. If it's other girls, and the yada, yada-ing turns into a "drag-a-girl-through-the mud" session, or a "can-you-believe-what-this-one-or-that-one did?" discussion, and lies and exaggeration appear for effect, then there's nothing harmless or innocent about it. We're gossiping.

Meantime, God is hanging his head. He's sad because he knows how temptation works: how gossip gives girls a false sense of importance and belonging; how girls think they'll be "in" when they tattle juicy scoops.

Okay, but we all like to talk. So, how do we know what's gossip and what's goofing around? Most of us can tell, but if there's any doubt, use the "Whatever" test. Ask yourself—

- Is it **true?** If we know something isn't true, or if we're not 100 percent sure, forget about it. "Hey, did you hear? The new girl got picked up by the cops the other day," Kelly told her friends. Later, a red-faced Kelly discovered the new girl's dad, a police officer, always picks her up after school on Wednesdays.

- And if it is true? Suppose the new girl *did* do something. Is it okay to blab gossip then? Or would it be more **noble/admirable** to say nothing? The Bible says, "A gossip betrays a confidence, but a trustworthy person keeps a secret" (Proverbs 11:13).

- Is spreading bad news about a girl the **right** thing to do? We've all done something we're not proud of. So let's not cast stones because we want to be center stage.

- Is it **pure?** We don't want to pass on impure gossip about another. This goes for an email, social media, and texts as well.

- Finally, if the gab is **lovely, excellent, or full of praise**, then by all means, we can yada, yada, yada until the sun comes up.

"So let us try to do what makes peace and helps one another," Paul said (Romans 14:19 NCV). Let's get rid of gossip.

Food for Thought

A woman gossiper was told to pluck a chicken, throw the feathers out the window, then go pick them up again. "I can't," she said. "So it is with gossip," the minister said. "You can't undo the damage your words did."

Second Thoughts

Gossip is one of the seven sins God despises. Read Proverbs 6:16–19 and find out the other six.

Divine Thoughts

Heavenly Father, sometimes putting other girls down makes me feel I'm better than they are. I need your help to remember how wrong that is. Amen.

Your Thoughts:

Devotion 65

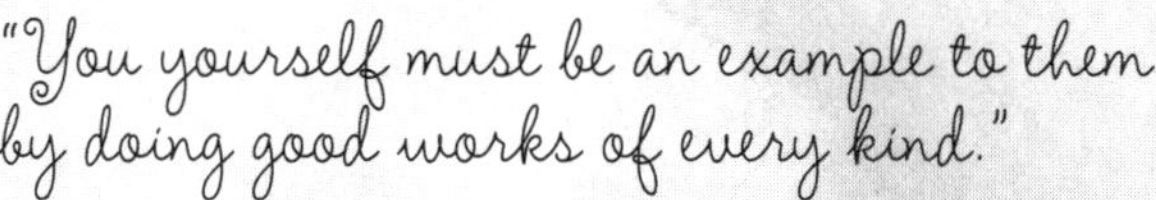

Titus 2:7 NLT

Just Like My Sister

Betty shooed her little sister, Libby, and Libby's BFF out of her room.

"Would you both just take a hike," she said impatiently. "I can't show you my new dress now, I'm texting."

Two days later, Libby was playing with her dolls when the dog waddled in.

"I'm having a tea party," Libby snapped at the poor pooch. "I don't have time to play with you. Go away!"

Little girls are, like, way impressionable. They think their big sisters are the absolute coolest. And, like little sponges, they soak up everything we do. That's why it's up to us, as someone they admire, to steer them in the right direction—to be a girl they can look up to and learn from.

In other words, be a good (God) example. The Bible says, "Christ suffered for you, leaving you an example, that you should follow in his steps" (1 Peter 2:21). So that's what we have to do: be a Christ-like role model in the way we talk, dress, and act. Here's how:

Show respect. Treat your sister like you'd want to be treated. Don't be bossy or talk down to her (1 Peter 5:3 MSG). Super busy? Explain nicely and make a date for later. Remember, Jesus was up to his eyeballs healing and preaching. But he still welcomed the children.

Be generous with your time and talents. Hang with your sister, get to know her, play, read, or do a project together. Use your God-given abilities—for painting, scrapbooking, martial arts, computers, soccer—to show your sister there's more to life than boys, clothes, and lip gloss.

Be careful how you dress. The Bible says, "glorify God in your body" (1 Corinthians 6:20 NRSV). So show your sister girls can look pretty and be popular without having to wear suggestive clothing, get tattooed and/or pierced, or slather on makeup.

Glamorize good behavior. Let your sister see that girls can be cool *and are cool,* when they do things like volunteer, act politely, get good grades, and are patient and kind. And, hopefully, it will rub off on her. Let her see you don't have to be a "bad girl" to get attention and love, and that it pleases God when you serve others instead of wanting to be served.

Our sisters look to us to be their heroes. So let's not let them down.

Food for Thought

The Bible says, "Direct your children onto the right path, and when they are older, they will not leave it" (Proverbs 22:6 NLT). So a good example's way important.

Second Thoughts

Being a role model helps you, too. Ask yourself, "Is this something I'd want my little sister to imitate?" when you're picking out clothes, and you'll be sure to pick the right ones.

Divine Thoughts

Jesus, I love my little sister and want to be a good example for her. Help me show her the right way. Amen.

Your Thoughts:

Devotion 66

"You intended to harm me, but God intended it for good to accomplish what is now being done, the saving of many lives."

Genesis 50:20

Lemonade from Lemons

What if your life suddenly spiraled out of control? What if your siblings tossed you in a pit, then sold you to some guys as a slave? And while at your new master's house, you were falsely accused, then got tossed into jail, forgotten, and left there to rot? Would you have a major meltdown? Feel God has turned his back on you? Want revenge?

Well, Joseph, the favorite son with the fancy coat, was only a teen when this seemingly unfortunate series of events dropped on him. Yet he had faith, kept his cool, and made lemonade from lemons. Let's see how he did it:

For starters, Joseph developed a strong faith at a young age, most likely due to his father, Jacob. As one of God's special friends, Jacob probably couldn't teach his children fast enough about the wonders of the Lord. So Joseph grew up with a solid foundation in the God of Abraham—the God who could always be trusted.

It's a lesson that stuck. Unlike his brothers, who just went through the motions, Joseph became a man who was "obviously filled with the spirit of God" (Genesis 41:38 NLT). So when things got tough, Joseph remained faithful.

He didn't dwell on the negative, either. When bad things happened, he didn't get whiney. Instead of thinking, *Why is this happening to me?* he trained himself to think, *How can I make this better?* Even as a slave, he worked hard and became the boss's favorite.

When he was thrown in jail for doing what was right (resisting Mrs. Potiphar), Joseph's super-sized faith kicked in again. He accepted what happened and looked for a way (with God's grace) he could control his circumstances—not let them control him. The result? His good behavior got him noticed by a man who'd ultimately get him released and into the Pharaoh's palace.

Finally, Joseph did something most of us probably could never imagine doing, given what he went through: He didn't seek revenge but forgave his brothers for trying to kill him.

Yup, we've got to admire Joseph on a bunch of different levels. But if we had to pick one out of the many things a faith like his teaches, it's this:

We never know when God is using us to further his plans for good. So we should make the best of *whatever* comes our way, and trust God *no matter what.*

Food for Thought

Joseph's story shows two things: that God can turn the evil others do around and use it for good and that his plans don't unfold overnight.

Second Thoughts

Joseph wasn't only admirable. He stood for *all* of the Whatever values. Read Genesis 37-50 and see if you can pick them out.

Divine Thoughts

Heavenly Father, when bad things happen and I don't know why, help me to remember Joseph and trust you. Amen.

Your Thoughts:

Devotion 67

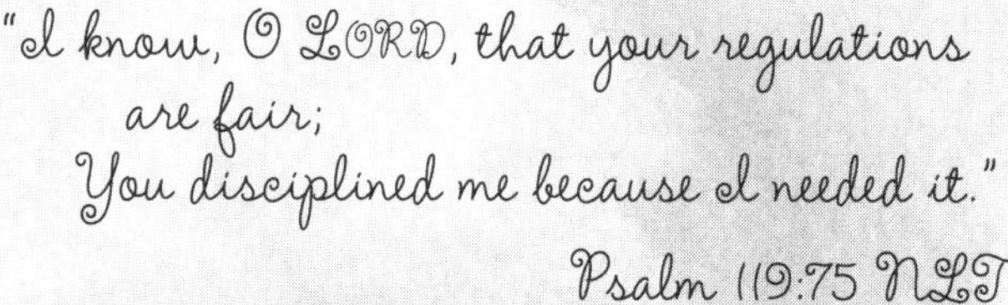

Taking Our Medicine

When we do something wrong and get caught, our very first thought is to act admirably, admit our mistake, and take our punishment.

NOT!

Okay, so we often try to wrangle our way out. We make excuses; we blame others. And sometimes, we act like the Drama Queen of the Year. We cry; we barter; we sulk. Very few of us get down on our knees and say, "Thanks, God. I needed that."

Too bad, because we should.

No question—being punished is a bummer. But it's also a blessing in disguise. It's God's way of tapping us on the shoulder and saying, "Ah, time to get back on the straight and narrow." He does this because he loves us and wants us to turn away from sin now (on earth) so we won't "face a fiery confrontation later" (1 Corinthians 11:32 MSG).

So the smart thing to do is to stop reacting and start reflecting and responding. Find a quiet place to sit, talk to God, listen for his answer, and make plans to improve. Writing stuff down in a journal helps. For instance, "I gave Betsy my homework. Then I lied to the teacher about it. I did it because I wanted her to like me. But if cheating and lying are what it takes for Betsy to notice me, then maybe it's better if I don't hang with Betsy."

Then pray for the Helper to send you the wisdom to learn from the experience, and the grace to change.

The writers of the Bible had a lot to say about discipline and, believe it or not, it was all positive: "My suffering was good for me, for it taught me to pay attention to your decrees" (Psalm 119:71). "God's discipline is always good for us" (Hebrews: 12:10 NLT). "It's the child he loves that [God] disciplines; the child he embraces, he also corrects" (Hebrews 12:6 MSG).

For sure, God does not want to lose any of us to sin. And if it takes a bit of "course correction" as a loving parent, he will do just that.

And we, in turn, can do the admirable thing: thank God for helping us recognize and admit where we're failing, take our medicine, and use it to grow closer to him.

Food for Thought

God often uses the same sin we committed to punish us—Jacob deceived his father, and his father-in-law deceived him. Read Genesis 27–29.

Second Thoughts

More good advice from the Bible: "My dear child, don't shrug off God's discipline, but don't be crushed by it either" (Hebrews 12:5 MSG).

Divine Thoughts

Heavenly Father, discipline stinks, but it also saves. Thanks God, for saving me and loving me so. Amen.

Your Thoughts:

Devotion 68

"Mary responded, 'I am the Lord's servant. May everything you have said about me come true.'"

Luke 1:38 NLT

No Excuses

If there were ever a girl who knew the right way to respond to God, it was Mary of Nazareth (aka Jesus's mom, who, BTW, was in her teens when she got that all-important call from God). Faced with a totally unbelievable proposal, delivered by a stranger appearing out of the blue, Mary remained unflustered, humble, and totally accepting.

Had she behaved in any other way, though, things would certainly have been iffy for all of us.

If she'd have said, "Um, you know, sir, maybe I'd better get back to you on this," or if she'd have replied, "Ah, I'll have to talk this over with my fiancé, Joseph," or if she'd have answered, "You know, I think I'll have to pass on this—they stone girls who wind up with child," the world would have been in a gi-normous mess. Our hope for redemption would have been up in the air.

But thanks to her courage, her no-hesitation, quick response, "I am willing," the entire world—every single man, woman, and child who accepts her Son, Jesus, from now until the end of time, is saved.

For sure, Mary acted admirably in a lot of ways:

- She didn't freak or run away. Instead, she stood bravely and listened to God's messenger.
- She didn't hesitate or give excuses. She didn't try to convince God she wasn't right for the job, like Moses (Exodus 4:10, 13). Or, like Jeremiah, she didn't say she was too young (Jeremiah 1:6).
- She never asked, "What do I get out of this?"
- She put God before her family, fiancé, community, reputation ... even her life.
- She didn't ask twenty questions (just one) before making her decision. The Lord God was giving her a mission—and no matter how impossible—she would take it on. End of story.

What about us? When God presents us with a special task, let's say, to invite a new girl to services, take part in a car-washing fundraiser, or teach little ones the Word, how do we respond? Are we too busy? Do we make excuses? Do we put God off?

Okay, if we did, well, that was the past. Today is the future. So let's show God we can be like Mary, too, and when he calls again, let's not even blink. Let's respond, "Whatever you want, Lord," without hesitation. "Let it be to me according to your word" (Luke 1:38 NKJV).

Food for Thought

Jesus compared God's kingdom to a great feast. Read the excuses some gave when the master invited them to this banquet in Luke 14:15-24 TLB.

Second Thoughts

Mary praised God for blessing her in a beautiful prayer called The Magnificat. Check it out in Luke 1:46-55.

Divine Thoughts

Dearest Jesus, like Mary, let me respond "Yes" to any plans you have for me. Amen.

Your Thoughts:

Section 8

Whatever's Excellent

Devotion 69

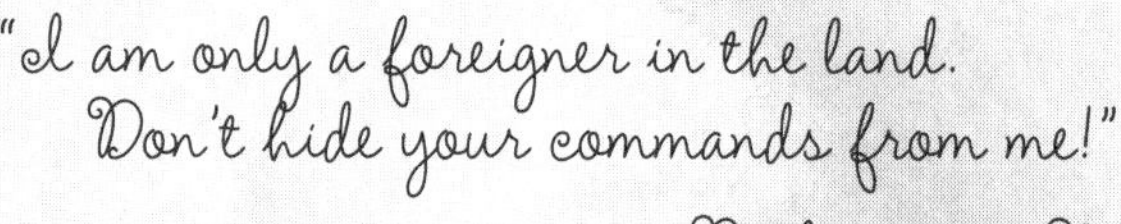

Rock-Solid Rules

Rules can be annoying. "Bathing caps MUST be worn in the pool." "TURN OFF All Cell Phones." "No DOGS Allowed." But imagine if we didn't have any? Our lives would be a mess, for sure.

God knew we needed rules in all areas of our lives. He could see that by the way people were acting. So, out of total love—and so we'd know about stuff like how to have a better relationship with him and others, what he expects from us, and what it takes to live a holy life—he laid down the law and gave it to Moses. We know it as the Ten Commandments.

Some girls think this Ten Commandments business is our Father's way of spoiling our fun. If they had read the Bible, though, they'd understand that's just not true. God gave us his Top Ten "for our own good," to protect us, and warn us away from harm (Deuteronomy 10:13 NLT) ... not to be a killjoy. Like any caring parent who'd tell her daughter, "Don't get in the car with someone who has been drinking," God gave us these rules to keep us safe.

Okay, so we're probably all familiar with the list itself. But here's some cool stuff that makes God's rules just as relevant now as they were when God first wrote them:

- They are right, clear, and give insight. They're not too hard. And those who follow them are happy (See Psalm 19:8; 1 John 5:3; Psalm 119:2).
- They're all about love, and the ten of them can be wrapped up into two: Love God with everything you've got, and love your neighbor as yourself. If we keep these two, we'll keep them all (Matthew 22:37-40).
- They're God's "final answer" to what's right and what's wrong. They're rock-solid; nothing can be added to or taken from them (Ecclesiastes 3:14).
- They can't save us from our sins. Only Jesus, who gave his life for us, can do that. But they show us how much we need Jesus as our Savior (Romans 3:20-28).

Jesus followed every single Top Ten rule and he wants us to as well. "If you love me," he said, "keep my commands" (John 14:15).

Food for Thought

Jesus takes the Ten Commandments a step further in the Beatitudes. Read them and see how in Matthew 5:17-48.

Second Thoughts

The Bible was written by men inspired by God. The Ten Commandments were written by the very hand of God himself (Deuteronomy 5:22).

Divine Thoughts

Dearest Jesus, when I'm confused about what's right or wrong, I can check out your rules. Like mom always says, "Read the directions first."

Your Thoughts:

Devotion 70

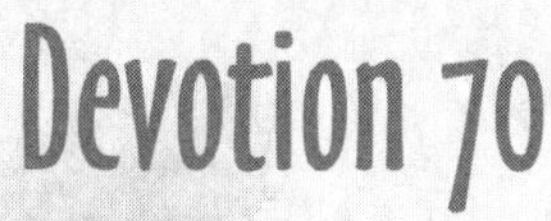

"Such things were written in the Scriptures long ago to teach us."

Romans 15:4 NLT

A Heavenly GPS

Some people say the Bible is like a love letter from God explaining how special we are to him and how much he loves us.

Other people say it's like an owner's manual—a book of instructions God has left to teach us how to live.

The Psalmist described God's Word as a "beam of light" that lets us see where we're going (Psalm 119:105 MSG).

If we had to make a comparison today, though, we might go techie, and say the Bible is like a "GPS" (a Global Positioning System—the kind some cars and phones have), because like a GPS, it gives us information we need to get us where we want to go.

Actually, the Bible as a "God Positioning System" isn't really all that far out when we think about what it does:

- It "is the power of God that brings salvation" (Romans 1:16).
- It keeps us from wandering "all over the place" (Psalm 119:67 MSG).
- It can get us back on the right road when we do make a wrong turn (Psalm 119:67 NLT).
- It acts as a guide (Psalm 119:19).
- It gives us a feeling of peace (Psalm 119:165).
- It's comforting (Psalm 119:52).

As our spiritual "God Positioning System," the Bible can do amazing things for us. In a letter to Timothy, Paul told him, "It corrects us when we are wrong and teaches us to do what is right" (2 Timothy 3:16 NLT). As most good GPSs do, it can also help us avoid toll roads that will cost us big and notify us of places we should avoid.

What's more, this GPS is the best on the planet and comes highly recommended by a man who has traveled this road himself, Jesus. Using it is way smarter than asking directions from girls who pretend to know where they're going, but wind up leading us down a dead-end road. Plus, we never have to worry about it breaking down because the manufacturer has warranted it with his life.

Paul said, "God uses [the Scriptures] to prepare and equip his people to do every good work" (2 Timothy 3:17 NLT).

So if we carry it with us every day, and refer to it often, chances are we'll never have trouble finding our way.

Food for Thought

What's so great about technology? You can get a phone App for the Bible (your spiritual GPS) and carry it in your purse. Awesome!

Second Thoughts

Heard about the Bible's Emergency Numbers? For help with bullies, try Psalm 27 when you're feeling lonely and frightened.

Divine Thoughts

Dear Jesus, when I'm lost, remind me to use my God Positioning System to find my way. Amen.

Your Thoughts:

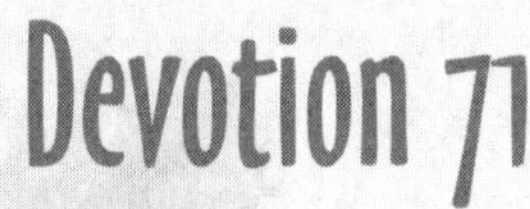

May you have the power to understand, as all God's people should, how wide, how long, how high, and how deep his love is."

Ephesians 3:18 NLT

God's Love: First, Free, Forever

You could spend your whole lifetime, and ten bazillion, gazillion lifetimes, thinking about God's love, and still have more to think about.

For now, though, let's check out these three points: God loved us first; God's love is free; and God's love is forever.

You're It...

God loved us first. He tagged you way before you even were "you," before your parents met, before Adam and Eve ate the apple. "Long before he laid down earth's foundations," the Bible says, "he had us in mind, had settled on us as the focus of his love" (Ephesians 1:4 MSG). And that's why we exist. But there's more: because God showed us how to love, now, it's our turn to love God back and to love our neighbor. "First we were loved, now we love" (1 John 4:19 MSG).

No Charge; No Strings

God's love is free. We can't buy it. We can't earn it. It's not based on whether we wear Tommy Hilfiger, or whether we're on the cheerleading team. God doesn't dole it out on the basis of us going to church, or being a perfect Christian. In fact, God loved us and sent his Son, Jesus, to save us even after we disobeyed him. "While we were still sinners, Christ died for us" (Romans 5:8).

What's more, God's love is "unconditional," which means there are no strings attached. God doesn't say, "Well, I'll love you, but only if you're kind to your mom," or "If you give to the poor, I'll love you even more." God's love doesn't work like that. Oh, and God loves us just the way we are, the unique individuals he made.

Endless Love

God's love is forever—the only kind that will last and last. It won't break. It won't spoil. You can't use it up. You can't lose it. Unlike earthly love, which has no guarantees, God's love is constant. What's more, nothing can get in the way of it. As Paul said, nothing can separate us from his love, "neither death nor life, neither angels nor demons, neither the present nor the future, nor any other powers" (Romans 8:38). And God himself tells us, "my unfailing love for you will not be shaken" (Isaiah 54:10).

One last thing: God will love you forever in heaven as

he does on earth. In fact, Jesus has gone to get your room ready (John 14:2–3). Cool, huh?

Food for Thought

The Bible says God has no favorites. He loves everyone the same. He "shows no partiality and cannot be bribed" (Deuteronomy 10:17 NLT).

Second Thoughts

Ever have a day when nothing goes right and everyone seems to be against you? That's the perfect time to think about how much God loves you.

Divine Thoughts

Jesus, there has never been a time when you didn't love me. There will never be a time when you don't. I love you, too. Amen.

Your Thoughts:

Devotion 72

"Provide purses for yourselves that will not wear out, a treasure in heaven that will never fail, where no thief comes near and no moth destroys."

Luke 12:33

The Really Good "Stuff"

Mention a totally excellent life, and the first thing many of us think of is being rich and having lots of "stuff"—designer clothes, jewelry, all the latest techie gadgets, and more.

Who can blame us? It's kind of hard *not* to think about stuff when everywhere we go, everyone is telling us we can never have enough of things we don't need.

As Christians, we have to work hard at blocking these messages, so we're not sucked into the Material Girl Syndrome, where what you have determines who you are.

"Life is not defined by what you have," Jesus said, "even when you have a lot" (Luke 12:15 MSG). Then he told a story about a foolish man who spent his life storing up grain and riches.

This guy was loaded with money, but his heart was as empty as a bank that just got robbed. Instead of thinking, *God has been good to me. I have so much. I should really share with people less fortunate,* his thoughts were only about himself. *How can I build more barns to store more grain*?

But God taught the man a costly lesson, and he died before he could enjoy his wealth. "Yes, a person is a fool to store up earthly wealth," Jesus said, "but not have a rich relationship with God" (Luke 12:21 NLT).

Jesus, the King of Kings, was not a flashy kind of guy. Though he could have had anything he wanted, he preferred to travel light—with just the clothes on his back. What's more, he encouraged his followers to leave all their possessions behind when he said, "Come, follow me" (Mark 1:17).

See, Jesus knows that earthly possessions get in people's way. He knows once we become too attached to earthly things, we put them before heavenly things.

That's what happened in another Bible story. A rich young man was so stuck on his possessions, he couldn't, wouldn't, and didn't give them up to follow Jesus (Mark 10:17-31). Boy, did he get short-changed. He could have been up in heaven, this very minute, living the totally excellent life with Jesus, but for his love of material stuff—things that have long since turned to dust.

So let's not settle for less. Let's put our possessions in perspective: If we have them, fine. If we don't, that's fine, too. Let's not let earthly stuff interfere with getting the most valuable "thing" around, what Jesus called a pearl of great value: eternal life (Matthew 13:45–46).

Food for Thought

Some rich and famous people have lots of stuff, but their souls aren't satisfied. Why? Because only God can satisfy. (Psalm 107:9).

Second Thoughts

Paul had the right idea. He said, "I'm just as happy with little as with much, with much as with little" (Philippians 4:12 MSG).

Divine Thoughts

Dearest Jesus, help me to control my longing for the new and cool stuff. Help me to keep my eyes on someone really excellent: you. Amen.

Your Thoughts:

Devotion 73

"Trust in the Lord with all your heart."

Proverbs 3:5

Falling in Trust with God

"Okay, everyone," Marla's youth minister said. "We're going to do a teamwork exercise: 'The Backwards Trust Game.'" Then he called for volunteers to be "fallers" and a bunch of kids to stand behind them and be "catchers."

Afterwards, he questioned the group: "Did anyone ask God to help her be more trusting before the game? Marla?"

"Not exactly," Marla answered. "But I did ask God to make sure these guys didn't drop me."

Trust means talking to God, telling him we know he's with us, and then believing he can help us through anything—even though we can't see him. As Christians, it's how we live. We're "sure of the things we hope for" and "that something is real even if we don't see it" (Hebrews 11:1 NCV). For us, it's not "seeing is believing" but "believing is seeing."

One word explains how we can do this: Jesus. He's proof positive that the Father exists because he, himself, is the

Father's reflection. Jesus confirmed that when he said, "Anyone who has seen me has seen the Father!" (John 14:9 NLT). The fact that the Father would send Jesus, his only Son, to die on the cross for our sins is also proof positive the Father loves us—a whole lot. And that's another reason why we trust God and his plans.

So what exactly *are* his plans? The Bible says they're plans to "prosper you and not to harm you, plans to give you hope and a future" (Jeremiah 29:11).

Cool. So we can expect pots of money, a fantastic job, and a totally excellent life?

Well, actually, no. Oh, we'll have life in abundance. God will shower us with blessings. He'll give us all we need here on earth (Ezekiel 34:26; John 10:10; 2 Peter 1:3). But his real plan—the hope and future the Bible talks about—is the free gift of a future with him in eternity (Romans 6:23). So once we accept Jesus, the path the Father's taking us down—the one we should trust whether we like, understand, or agree with it—is always leading us towards that end.

That's why trust is so totally excellent. The more we have of it, the easier it is for us to let go (of what we think should be happening), and let God (work things out for our benefit). Because eternity's not something we can see right now either. It's something we just have to trust God on and take his word for.

Food for Thought

The Bible's full of people who had faith in God under really scary circumstances. Read a sampling in Hebrews 11.

Second Thoughts

The better we know someone, the more we trust him/her. So get to know God better by praying, spending quiet time with him, and reading his Word.

Divine Thoughts

Dearest Jesus, when I don't understand things that are happening, and I'm afraid, help me to trust you. Amen.

Your Thoughts:

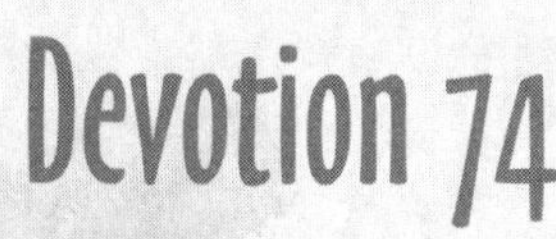

Devotion 74

"These trials will show that your faith is genuine."

1 Peter 1:7 NLT

Making the Grade

Tests. Nobody likes 'em. But they're a fact of life. Teachers use them to find out how much we've learned and whether the stuff we've been taught is sticking. God uses them to strengthen our trust, check our obedience, and see how our faith holds up when things get hairy.

Take Noah, for example. He was tested in "Faith Under Pressure and Ridicule," "Ark Building 101," and "Trust While Traveling Through Scary Storms and Floods." While everyone around him hinted that he had stayed out in the sun too long, Noah ignored them, obeyed God, and then, "By his faith ... he received the righteousness that comes by faith" (Hebrews 11:7 NLT). In other words, Noah aced his exams.

God used the son Abraham had waited for his whole lifetime to prove Abraham's obedience quotient. And he came through this trial with flying colors. He was willing to obey

God even if it meant offering his son Isaac to die on the altar (James 2:21 TLB).

Then there were Joseph, Moses, Joshua, David, Daniel, Job, Jonah, Mary, Joseph, Peter, and Paul—honor students all.

How'd they do it? The Bible says it was by "faith" (Hebrews 11:8). When they faced trials, they didn't think, This is too hard. I can't do it. Instead they thought, *I don't know where this is leading, but I do know God is loving, powerful, and trustworthy. So I'm with him.*

That's a good study plan for us to follow. If "We live by faith, not by sight" (2 Corinthians 5:7), we'll be ready to trust God unconditionally—even if our BFF ditches us, we break a leg in soccer, or some other nasty thing comes our way.

Easy? Nope. But we can't expect to prove or learn anything if the test is a snap. Yet the Bible reassures us that our trials won't be off the charts either, as God "will never let you be pushed past your limit; he'll always be there to help you come through it" (1 Corinthians 10:13 MSG).

And the good news is that each time we rely on God's help when our world seems messed up, or we're confused about what's happening, we exercise our trust muscles and our faith grows stronger.

P.S.: The Bible says, "God blesses those who patiently endure testing and temptation. Afterward they will receive the crown of life that God has promised to those who love him" (James 1:12 NLT).

What size crown will He save for you?

Food for Thought

Read how Shadrach, Meshach, and Abednego passed their test—a real-life fiery one in Daniel 3:8-30.

Second Thoughts

"If we are unfaithful, he remains faithful, for he cannot deny who he is" (2 Timothy 2:13 NLT).

Divine Thoughts

Dear God, help me to trust that your love will see me through any trial or problem. Amen.

Your Thoughts:

Devotion 75

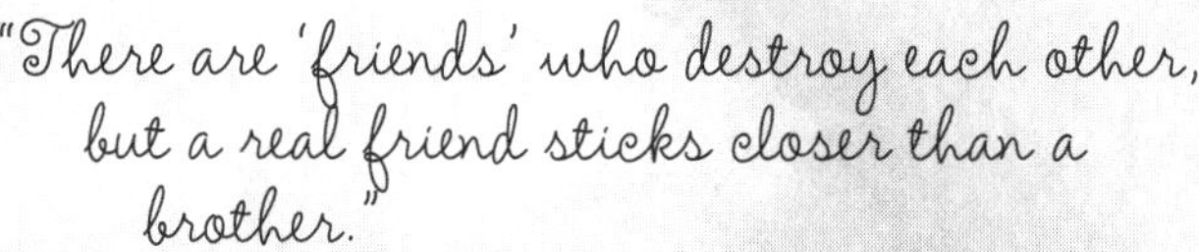
"There are 'friends' who destroy each other, but a real friend sticks closer than a brother."

Proverbs 18:24 TLB

The Right Friends

Hannah, the head cheerleader, was popular with the other girls, until she fell, broke her leg, and wound up in a cast and on the sidelines. Her teammates were sympathetic at first. But soon, they rushed passed her with nothing but a nervous wave. Everybody was too busy getting to know the new girl who took her place. Everybody that is except her BFF, Emily.

"I feel so alone, Em," Hannah said. "Thank God, you're not ignoring me, too."

Friends—real friends—are an awesome gift from the Lord. Like our heavenly BFF, Jesus, the totally excellent ones hang with us through thick and thin. They lift us up when we're low. They take our part when others shut us out. "A friend loves at all times" (Proverbs 17:17).

The Bible says, "If one [person] falls down, the other

helps ... By yourself, you're unprotected. With a friend you can face the worst" (Ecclesiastes 4:10, 4:10, 12 MSG).

Finding the right BFFs, though, can be tricky. All sorts of people want to "friend" us on Facebook and Twitter. But off line, for believers, it's quality not quantity that counts. We need buddies who'll share our faith and help us grow closer to Jesus.

So we need to choose BFFs *very carefully*. The Bible says love everyone, but "Don't become partners with those who reject God" (2 Corinthians 6:14 MSG). It's a recipe for disaster. If we get real chummy with a girl who doesn't believe in Jesus and doesn't want to know about him, we'll disagree on everything—from prayer and going to church, to music, clothes, and movies. Even worse, we may be tempted to start tiptoeing around God to avoid being "too religious."

Finding the right BFFs, though, is awesome. They can not only giggle and cry with us, plan and dream with us, they can also watch our spiritual backs. The Bible says, "As iron sharpens iron, so a friend sharpens a friend" (Proverbs 27:17 NLT). And that's what a good BFF does. If we're struggling with gossiping or cussing and we slip, she can nudge us. What's more, we can feel at ease around her when we pray, read the Word, or worship.

Once we've found that totally excellent friend, how do we keep her? Be a totally excellent friend back, like the best one we'll ever have: Jesus.

Food for Thought

Where can you find totally excellent friends? In a chat room? On Facebook? In church? Where do you think?

Second Thoughts

Jesus hung with sinners—to bring them to his Father. They couldn't influence him (he's God). But *he* sure did influence them.

Divine Thoughts

Dearest Lord, help me to find friends who love you as much as I do. Amen.

Your Thoughts:

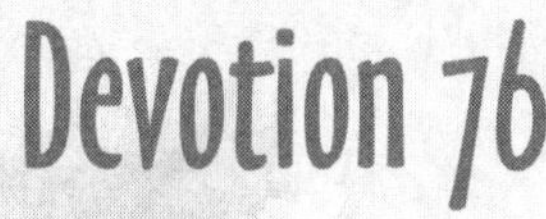

"Instead I have calmed and quieted myself, like a weaned child who no longer cries for its mother's milk. Yes, like a weaned child is my soul within me."
Psalm 131:2 NLT

Chillaxing

"Take it easy," Justine's mom said when Justine lost her purse. But that's the last thing she could do. *My whole life's in that bag,* she thought. *My school pass, my brand new raspberry lip gloss. OH, NO, and my phone!"*

Justine borrowed her mom's cell and ran off to retrace her steps, while at the same time, yakitty-yaking with her BFF about how this was such a disaster, and how she'd just die if she didn't get the bag back. She was so frazzled, she forgot half the stores she'd been in and was going around in circles. Finally, she slumped down on a bench and cried.

When something difficult, terrible, or awful happens, do you totally freak? Do you get unhinged? Yeah, we all do. It's, like, our minds take off in a million different directions. We get so upset—we're useless.

The Bible has a simple, but effective, eight-word remedy for this: "Be still, and know that I am God" (Psalm 46:10).

See, we can't accomplish anything if we're in a state of emergency.

So the first thing we need to do is stop, get quiet and calm, and let go of our need to do something immediately to solve the problem. That's the "be still" part.

The second part is the "knowing," and that's easier because we already "know" God. We know he's loving and kind. We know he's more powerful than any problem we have. We know he has come through for us in the past. We know the Word says he works everything out for our good if we love him (Romans 8:28), and that his power works best when we're weak (2 Corinthians 12:9 NLT).

So putting those two elements together—being still and knowing God—can help us simmer down, get a grip, and remind ourselves to trust more and panic less. "Be silent before the LORD," the Word advises, "for he is springing into action from his holy dwelling" (Zechariah 2:13 NLT).

That's God's job—to spring into action. Our job is to stay calm, remember he can handle anything, then step out of the way, and let him.

P.S.: Justine's bag was turned in to security by a girl who left this note: "I'd have been so bummed if I lost my bag. Was so happy to be able to return yours." Did the Holy Spirit nudge her? You think?

Food for Thought

The army opposing Jehoshaphat was huge. His message to God? "Help!" God's reply, "stand still and watch the Lord's victory." Read more in 2 Chronicles 20:1–30.

Second Thoughts

No matter where you are, you can get yourself "still" by saying the short Jesus Prayer: "Lord, Jesus Christ, Son of God, have mercy on me, a sinner."

Divine Thoughts

Heavenly Father, please help me to always remember you're in control and have everything under control. Amen.

Your Thoughts:

Devotion 77

"I consider everything a loss because of the surpassing worth of knowing Christ Jesus my Lord, for whose sake I have lost all things."

Philippians 3:8

Knowing Jesus

"Oh, look at that one, Steph!" Dolly said as she ogled engagement rings. "It's like totally excellent."

"This one's better, Dee," Stephanie said. "It's like way sparkly."

"Whoa! You're right," Dolly said. "I need my sunglasses!"

"It's a genuine diamond," the saleswoman said. "The other is a cubic zirconium."

There's nothing like the real thing, and once we know the difference, nothing compares. And that includes the stuff of the world versus knowing and serving Jesus. Some girls may think popularity, fitting in, money, fame, and success are totally excellent (and they are to some extent). But put that stuff alongside Jesus—like the zirconium vs. the real diamond—and it just doesn't measure up. Let's make a list and see:

Some of What Knowing Jesus Offers:

- By his suffering and death, Jesus made us right with God; he paid for our sins (Romans 3:25).
- Jesus will never jilt or abandon us. He'll always love us (John 10:28).
- When trouble comes our way, Jesus stands by us and gives us courage to get through it (Psalm 46:1).
- Jesus strengthens and keeps us safe, showers us with blessings, and gives us peace (2 Thessalonians 3:3; Ephesians 1:3; John 14:27).
- With Jesus, we have life to the fullest here and the promise of eternal life (with new, improved bodies) in his Father's house (John 10:10; John 17:1-3; Philippians 3:21; John 14:2).

Some of What the World Offers:

- Popularity which will only last until someone who girls like better comes along.
- Acceptance by the in-crowd, but the price can be as high as gossiping or cheating. P.S.: We can be accepted today, though, then dumped tomorrow.
- Money that can buy us things which will eventually be dated, worn out, broken, or rotted (and could get stolen).
- Fame which feels empty after a while and, like popularity, only lasts until the new super-star appears.

See, once we know Jesus—what he's done for us and what he does for us—nothing else even comes close. Nothing else is as good as the Alpha and the Omega, the totally excellent, genuine, real Son of God—the only one who can satisfy us completely. And when we know Jesus, for sure, *there's nothing else* we need.

Food for Thought

Wouldn't the world be a totally excellent place if everyone could come to know Jesus? Put that on your prayer list.

Second Thoughts

We can get to know God better by reading the long letter he gave us: The Bible.

Divine Thoughts

Dear Jesus, nothing compares to the joy of knowing you. Amen.

Your Thoughts:

Section 9

Whatever's Praiseworthy

Devotion 78

"We cannot stop telling about everything we have seen and heard."

Acts 4:20 NLT

An Expert Witness

Mercy had it in for JayCee. She called her a dweeb because JayCee loved math and made fun of the fact that she was a Christian.

"So, where was your God on 9/11?" Mercy jeered. "Out to lunch, like you?"

"Let's talk about it," JayCee said, but Mercy walked off. Then the unthinkable happened: Mercy was failing in math. So the teacher asked JayCee to be her study partner.

Working with JayCee closely and seeing her live out her faith in little ways left an impression on Mercy. She still made fun of JayCee every chance she got. But three months later, she asked her if she could drop in on youth group to, "Check out this Jesus dude."

Jesus told us to "Go into all the world and preach the Good News to everyone" (Mark 16:15 NLT). There are dozens of ways we can do that and a bunch of things to keep in mind. Here are just a few:

Like JayCee, we can witness without words—spread the Good News by showing rather than telling. If we say, "Jesus wants us to treat others the way we want to be treated," some girls may roll their eyes. But if these girls actually see us being nice to someone who's mean to us, they'll wonder why we're not being mean back. When they ask, we can explain.

Girls are more receptive to people they know and trust. So it's better to friend a person before trying to introduce her to Jesus.

Don't know the answer to a challenge? Say, "Good question; I'll check it out and get back to you." Then do just that—get the info, write it down, and share it.

Give those who're curious what's important first: Christ loves us; he died for our sins; he rose from the dead; and if we accept him as our Savior, we're saved. We have eternal life.

Though being passionate about witnessing is praiseworthy, we need to know when to disengage. When girls get nasty or hostile, it's time to say, "Sorry you feel this way," and leave.

Expert witnesses know their subject. So, obviously, the more we learn about Jesus, the better our testimony.

Finally, it goes without saying, an expert witness needs to be "Spirited," full of the Spirit. Because when all is said and done, only with the Helper's grace can we plant the seed. And he's the only one who can make it grow.

Food for Thought

Got "witness jitters?" Don't worry. Jesus said he "will give you the right words and such wisdom that none of your opponents will be able to reply or refute you!" (Luke 21:15 NLT).

Second Thoughts

You can be a powerful witness by sharing a struggle you yourself have had, say, with lying or anger, and how God is working with you to change.

Divine Thoughts

Jesus, please send your Spirit to help me spread the word about you everywhere. Amen.

Your Thoughts:

Devotion 79

"O LORD, our Lord,
your majestic name fills the earth!
Your glory is higher than the heavens."

Psalm 8:1 NLT

Holy Is God's Name

"Oh my God! Oh my God!" Camille squeals at her BFF in the mall. "That sweater. It's, like, like, perfect for the skirt I bought last week."

"Oh ... my ... God," Paola says to her mother, drawing out the words. "You can't be serious? You're not *really* taking away my phone, are you?"

"Oh my God, not again." Vanessa says as her little brother barges into her room for the umpteenth time.

Tossing God's name around in vain, without thinking, happens all the time. The phrase "Oh my God" (OMG in text-talk) in particular seems to have crept into the national vocabulary. We hear it on TV, in movies, and videos, and see it on the Internet in the zillion texts that go back and forth all day.

Lots of girls use it automatically as a systematic response

to being surprised, angry, disgusted, or bored. Some girls even say OMG for no good reason, a mindless conversation opener in place of, "Hey," or "Did you hear this?"

But OMG is, like, just an expression. Right? It's not really using God's name in vain. God knows we don't mean it in a bad way. It's just a figure of speech.

Wrong. Using the holy name of the Lord when we're not praising, petitioning, singing worship songs, or talking to God is not showing him the respect he deserves. It's like calling on God for no reason. And God minds very much, because when we say his name offhandedly, we break his law. "Do not misuse the name of the LORD your God," the Bible tells us in the third commandment. If you do, expect consequences. "The LORD will not let you go unpunished" (Exodus 20:7 NLT).

On top of that, as Christians, it doesn't seem right for us to go to church and worship God, then step outside and disrespect him in the parking lot. "Out of the same mouth come praise and cursing," the Bible warns us yet again. "This should not be" (James 3:10). And the "everybody does it" excuse doesn't cut it, because God has set us apart to lead others in doing good, not so we can follow them into evil.

Okay, so let's keep the holy name of God holy. Let's bite our tongue rather than use it in a careless way. God wants us to call him OMG, but in praise and worship. That's the only place those words belong.

Food for Thought

Think about when and why you use the OMG expression, and try to remove yourself from those kinds of situations.

Second Thoughts

Instead of OMGing, come up with a different expression: "Oh great gummieworms," or "Great golly gee." Be creative.

Divine Thoughts

Lord, I'm really sorry for OMGing you. I know I sometimes use some other words I shouldn't, too. Help me, Lord, watch what I say. Amen.

Post Script

The fact that "OMG" has made it into the dictionary proves how wide-spread the expression is. But that STILL doesn't mean it's okay for Christian Whatever girls to use.

Your Thoughts:

Devotion 80

*"Not to us, O LORD, not to us
but to your name goes all the glory
for your unfailing love and
faithfulness."*

Psalm 115:1 NLT

Do the Deed; Skip the Praise

Charise's church group volunteered at several seniors' homes around town. Charise came, raked up a few leaves, and left early. Then she blogged about how "helping one's neighbor" meant so much to her. A reporter saw the blog and interviewed her for a piece on "Tweens and Volunteerism." Her BFFs high-fived her for being in the paper. Her parents and relatives thought she was another Mother Teresa. God saw through her, though, and knew she was all about the applause.

"Be careful not to practice righteousness in front of others to be seen by them," Jesus said (Matthew 6:1). Instead when you give, pray, or fast, do it privately, without fanfare. "Then your Father, who sees what is done in secret, will reward you" (Matthew 6:6).

See, the motive behind good works is to give God glory and help others. So when we do something praiseworthy, it's really between God and us—nobody else needs to know. Otherwise, we risk becoming "Do-Gooder-Showoffs" like the Pharisees. They "loved human praise more than the praise of God" (John 12:43 NLT). And talk about attention-seekers! They strapped on super-sized prayer boxes filled with Scripture and wore gi-normous tassels to make people believe they were reverencing the Ten Commandments.

But it was all for show. They didn't practice what they preached. They did good deeds for their own glory. They walked around with an "I am holier than you'll ever be" attitude. Jesus saw the danger of acting this way and gave us instructions to avoid it. When we give to the poor, he said, don't "announce it with trumpets" (Matthew 6:2). When we pray, do it in private, "go into your room, close the door" (Matthew 6:6). And when we fast, don't walk around "miserable and disheveled" so we look like martyrs (Matthew 6:16 NLT).

Okay, but shouldn't we shine our light so we can bring others to Christ by our actions? You betcha. But that's more likely to happen if girls see us doing good deeds in a low-key, not-for-our-own-profit way than it is if they catch us acting generous to prop up our good-girl image.

"As the Scriptures say, 'If you want to boast, boast only about the Lord'" (2 Corinthians 10:17 NLT).

When it comes to good works, that about says it all.

Food for Thought

Jesus brought Lazarus back from death, "for the glory of God" (John 11:4 NLT). Mostly, though, he healed people and told them not to tell anybody.

Second Thoughts

Praise for doing what you should? Sorry. "When you obey me," Jesus said, "you should say, 'We are unworthy servants who have simply done our duty'" (Luke 17:10 NLT).

Divine Thoughts

Dearest Jesus, I admit it: sometimes I crave recognition. So help me to do good, then forget about it … because I know you won't. Amen.

Your Thoughts:

Devotion 81

"Dear children, keep yourselves from idols."

1 John 5:21

Putting God First

Ofelia loved soccer. She walked, talked, lived, and breathed the game. Her bedroom was a shrine to the U.S. Women's Olympic Soccer Team. To say she was a soccer freak was putting it mildly.

"I signed up for VBS," her friend Tammy said. "You going?"

"Nah," Ofelia replied. "I'm doing soccer camp instead. I had to practically beg my parents. But they gave in, finally. I'm so excited, I can't stand it."

Neither can God. We can hear him now: "Moses, they're at it again—worshipping false gods. Something called soccer this time. And Ofelia prefers that to me!"

Okay, so we'd never dream of kneeling down to a golden cow. Yet some girls make and worship their own modern-day idols. They push God aside, put something or someone else in his place, and let these false gods control their thoughts and impact their decisions.

For some, it's material things like clothes or techy gadgets. Others make idols of rock stars or movie and TV celebrities. Still others worship at the altar of beauty, popularity, money, success, acceptance, or sports.

Does that mean we can't be interested in fashion and technology, or be movie star fans, or join cheerleading club?

Of course not. What we're talking about here is being so involved in something that we rob God of his rightful portion of our time, energy, love, and enthusiasm. (Like when we blow off church services to go to a concert or spend four hours on social media and skip reading the Bible.) It's when we look to something or someone other than God to satisfy our needs. The Bible calls this worshipping "the things God created instead of the Creator himself, who is worthy of eternal praise!" (Romans 1:25 NLT).

"Do not make any gods to be alongside me" (Exodus 20:23), God warns, and he means it. God detests idolatry. The Bible is full of references of him demanding idols be smashed, burnt, and destroyed (Exodus 23:24; Deuteronomy 7:5; 2 Chronicles 15:8).

Okay, so what takes priority in our thoughts and our hearts?

If it's anyone or anything but the Lord, we need to change our lifestyles, trash the false idols, and do the praiseworthy thing—put God back where he belongs, up front and center stage.

Food for Thought

God made his position very clear in the first commandment: "You shall have no other gods before me" (Exodus 20:3).

Second Thoughts

Stars some girls idolize can fall off their pedestals and get tossed aside by the world. Let's pray for them.

Divine Thoughts

Dear God, I admit that sometimes I put other things ahead of you. I know this hurts you and I'm sorry. Amen.

Your Thoughts:

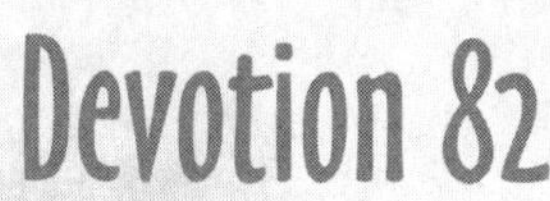

Devotion 82

"... don't be stuck-up. Make friends with nobodies; don't be the great somebody."

Romans 12:16 MSG

A Humble Heart

Adele's thumbs flew across the keyboard as she excitedly texted all her friends: "I'm a Brown Belt! Yay!!" When she bumped into Paige, the new girl, she even told her.

"Wow," Paige said. "That's awesome. Congrats. I'd love to come to your Dojo and watch you some time."

Now Paige, a karate expert with dozens of trophies to her name, could have spoiled Adele's day with one sentence: "Been there, done that, black belt, five-time champion." Instead she did a self-effacing and praiseworthy thing: she shared in Adele's joy and kept her own achievements to herself.

Seems Paige not only knows karate, she also knows how to be humble. And today it's harder and harder to find girls who are. That's because the world encourages a "Look-what-I've-done-I'm-better-than-you" attitude, and a lot of girls buy into it. They spend gazillions of hours on social media playing the one-upmanship game and bragging about themselves.

Okay, so we all feel good when we've accomplished something. And we obviously want to share. Problem is, some girls get carried away. They spend so much time telling everyone how great they are, they begin to believe it.

The Bible says when our hearts become proud, we're so full of ourselves, there's no room for the Lord (Psalm 10:4). And that's exactly what happens. Instead of thanking God ten times to Sunday for his abundant grace, proud girls start believing they—not God—are responsible for the good stuff that comes their way. The result? (Unlike Paige) they look down on everyone and act like total divas.

Paul warned the Corinthians about this: "What gives you the right to make such a judgment? What do you have that God hasn't given you? And if everything you have is from God, why boast as though it were not a gift?" (1 Corinthians 4:7 NLT).

It is a reminder that everything—our looks, talents, and skills—comes directly from God, as a gift, on loan, for our temporary use. And as for being superior, Paul told his followers, "Do nothing out of selfish ambition or vain conceit. Rather, in humility value others above yourselves" (Philippians 2:3).

Paul was big on humility because Jesus was. And if the King of Kings can come down from heaven, demand no privileges, give all the glory to his Father, and serve others, we can, too.

Food for Thought

God doesn't want you to minimize your talents or put yourself down. He just wants you to remember where your blessings come from.

Second Thoughts

Jesus tried to teach people about humility with his life and with his parables. Read John 13:12-17; Luke 14:7-14; 18:9-14.

Divine Thoughts

Heavenly Father, help me to remember to be humble, and put you first, others second, and myself last. Amen.

Your Thoughts:

Devotion 83

*"Let my mouth be filled with Your praise
And with Your glory all the day."*
Psalm 71:8 NKJV

Praise Days

Praise is an important part of how we communicate with God. But we don't have to go away on a special retreat to be able to get our message across. Nope. We can actually spend our days in praise anywhere because everything we do, if we do it in appreciation, celebration, and adoration of who God is and what he's done for us—can be an act of praise.

The Bible says we were born for praise (Isaiah 43:21), and that we're to do it "From the rising of the sun to its going down" (Psalm 113:3 NKJV). What's more, the Psalmists (who were big into praise) said we're to do it "with all my inmost being" (Psalm 103:1), our heart, our soul, and our body.

So we can praise God in the traditional ways—with prayer, hymns, and music. Or we can do something a little different, like start a praise blog with photos and poems, or an "I Praise You" journal with daily entries of admiration, or even a "Praise Through Our Days" social media fan page. In fact, anything—art, dance, photography, volunteering, reading Scriptures, or a fast from TV or texting—can be a form of praise.

Thing to remember here, though, is praise is all about God. So we have to put our own needs and wants on the back burner and concentrate completely on him. We have to let God sit back while we compliment him, rave about him, and tell him just how phantasmagorical, mighty, merciful, just, kind, patient, holy, powerful, full of loving kindness, magnificent, and just plain totally awesome he is—and how much we adore him. That's the kind of praise session that'll get God's attention.

The Bible says we should "worship God in a way that will please him, with reverence and awe" (Hebrews 12:28 TEV). And when God's pleased, some unbelievable things happen. For example, after Paul and Silas sang hymns and prayed to the Lord (Acts 16:25–26), an earthquake shook the prison and opened the locked cells. And after King Jehoshaphat sent singers ahead of his army to sing and praise the Lord, God won a gi-normous battle without Jehoshaphat lifting a finger (2 Chronicles 20:22).

God can, has, and will do some pretty unbelievable things in our lives, too. For that, and well, just because he is who he is, let's not only spend our days but also our whole lives praising him to the high heavens.

Food for Thought

David really had a way with words. See how beautifully he praises God in Psalms 145 to 150.

Second Thoughts

Whenever we talk to God for whatever reason, it's always a good idea to start and end with praise.

Divine Thoughts

Heavenly Father, a lot of times when I pray, it's all about me. From now on, I want to have regular sessions when it's all about you. Amen.

Your Thoughts:

Devotion 84

"Use the gift you have."

1 Timothy 4:14 NCV

Got Talents? Use 'Em

Laura's parents were having their 10th anniversary party. So Laura learned the song they danced to at their wedding reception and sang it as a surprise.

"You have a lovely voice," Laura's aunt said later. "You should try out for the choir. They're looking for girls."

"Thanks, Aunt Mary," Laura said. "I'll think about it."

And she did ... for all of five minutes. *Well,* she thought, *I wouldn't mind singing in the choir. The girls are pretty nice. But practice is on Mondays, so no bowling club. And I'll have to be at church early, so no sleeping in. Then I'll have to learn to read music and be available on holidays. Choir sounds way too much like work. I think I'll pass.*

Laura may not have realized it. But she just talked herself into burying her talents in the ground, like the "do nothing" servant in Jesus' parable (Matthew 25:14-30). You know, the one who didn't use what was given to him. And when the master returned to settle accounts, he praised the other servants for their work. But he called that guy "worthless" (Matthew 25:30).

The Bible says, "God in his kindness gave each of us different gifts" (Romans 12:6 GWT). And obviously, it was for a reason: He wants us to use them. How? In service to him—to build up his kingdom on earth. And we need to get moving. Because when Jesus returns, like the master in the parable, he will have his clipboard out and demand an accounting:

"I gave you a beautiful voice," he'll say. "Did you use it to praise me? Or just to amuse your friends by mimicking some popular rock star?"

"I gave you a writer's flair," he'll say. "Did you spend any time blogging about my Father? Or waste it all on social media gossip?"

"I gave you a brain for teaching," he'll say. "Did you use it to instruct little ones about my love? Or was your calendar too filled with other, cooler stuff?"

Only the Father knows when Jesus will come back to judge how we used our gifts. So let's get ourselves ready now so he won't have to check any columns marked "Not Interested," "Too Lazy," or "Afraid of What Others Think/Say."

Let's make sure all the checkmarks are in the "Praiseworthy," "Good work," "Well Done," and "Good and Faithful Servant" columns instead.

Food for Thought

In the parable of the talents, the master wasn't upset the one servant didn't do as well as the others; he was angry that the servant totally blew him off and did nothing.

Second Thoughts

If you don't know what your special talent is yet, ask God to help you find it. Meantime, use the gifts you do have—youth, energy, and time—to honor him.

Divine Thoughts

Jesus, you've blessed me with so much. Keep me from wasting my talents; help me to use them to serve you. Amen.

Your Thoughts:

Devotion 85

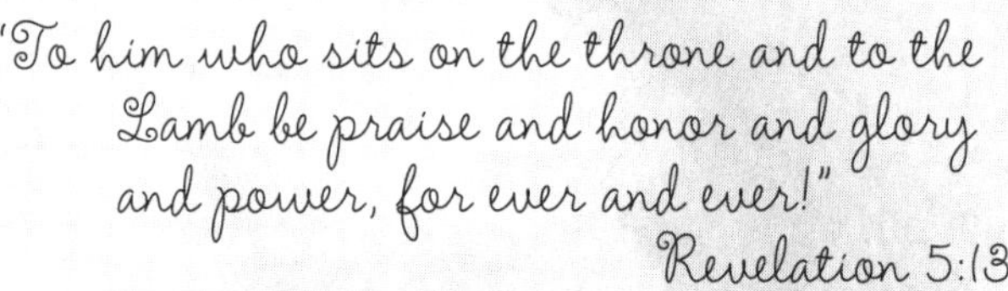

The Lamb Who Was Slain

We could probably never imagine stepping in and taking someone else's punishment. Okay, maybe we might do it for a really, really good BFF, or someone we really, really loved. But if someone asked us to die for them—especially someone we didn't know, or someone who'd been mean to us, or just plain ignored us—well, that would be a different story altogether.

The Bible says, "Now it is an extraordinary thing for one to give his life even for an upright man, though perhaps for a noble and lovable and generous benefactor someone might even dare to die" (Romans 5:7 AMP).

Yet Jesus, the Lamb who was slain, did just that. He was totally innocent but stood in and took the blame for our sins. He suffered and died in our place. And he did this "while we were still sinners" (Romans 5:8). In other words,

Jesus didn't say to his Father, "Okay, once these people stop sinning, apologize, and ask for forgiveness, then I'll go down and sacrifice myself for them." Nope. While we were still estranged from God, while we were still ignoring him and breaking his laws—that's when Jesus shed his blood to make things right between God and us. And that was, by far, *the* most praiseworthy thing anybody ever did: "He was pierced through for our transgressions, He was crushed for our iniquities," and "by His scourging we are healed" (Isaiah 53:5 NASB).

The physical pain was excruciating. But the mental anguish was equally bad. Remember this was the Father's beloved Son. Yet to be able to fully atone for our sins, Jesus had to become sin. The Father had to turn his back on him, totally cut himself off, abandon Jesus. And Jesus had to bear that, too.

For sure, there really only should be a one-word description of the word "praiseworthy" in the dictionary: "Jesus." Without a doubt, there is no one more worthy of the honor—which is why the Father exalted him to the highest place in heaven where, at just the mention of his name, all knees bow and all tongues proclaim him Lord (Philippians 2:10–11). So let's add our voices to that mighty chorus and say: "Worthy is the Lamb, who was slain, to receive power and wealth and wisdom and strength and honor and glory and praise!" (Revelation 5:12).

Food for Thought

Jesus—the Lamb who was slain—is the only person worthy to open the scroll that has God's plans for the last days. Read about it in Revelation 5:1-14.

Second Thoughts

A great way to begin prayer is to say "hallelujah" ("halelu-Yah") which means "Praise the Lord!" See how it's used in Psalm 104:35, Psalm 111:1, and Revelation 19:1.

Divine Thoughts

Jesus, Lord, I praise you and love you and thank you for what you did, now and always. Amen.

Your Thoughts:

Devotion 86

"But just as he who called you is holy, so be holy in all you do; for it is written: 'Be holy, because I am holy.'"

1 Peter 1:15–16

Answering the Call

Quiz time—holiness means: (a) never using lipstick; (b) fasting three days a week; (c) reading Scripture on street corners.

None of the above. You got it. But since leading a holy life is praiseworthy—something Scripture says God's calling us to do—let's check it out.

Okay, so why be holy anyway? Three important reasons: God tells us to; we love him and want to please him; and because "those who are not holy will not see the Lord" (Hebrews 12:14 NLT). And yes, there are a lot of ideas on what the key is, but in a nutshell, the way to holiness is by association with, imitation of, and dedication to Jesus.

See, Jesus is in and of himself holy because he is God, and we are holy in him—he shares his holiness with us through the blood of his cross which sanctifies us and his Spirit which transforms us.

The second part—imitating Jesus—figures in this way: The word "holy" means "to be separate," to be "set apart." And that's how Jesus behaved when he came to earth. He was in the world but "set apart," or "separated" from it. He stayed pure among the impure. He mingled with the proud and acted humble. He ate with sinners and was blameless.

So if we want to answer God's call to be holy, we have to copy Jesus; "walk just as he walked" (1 John 2:6 NRSV). Like he did, we have to have one foot in this world, but our eyes fixed on the next.

That's some balancing act, for sure. But God wouldn't put out this call without a way for us to answer. So he's provided tools—the changing power of the Holy Spirit (who makes us holy), the gift of his Word, and Jesus's example. We need only supply one thing: commitment. We have to make a decision, now, to separate ourselves from what's sinful—the things others swear are cool, trendy, and way awesome—and then stick with it. (Thinking Whatever thoughts can help.)

Oh, and be prepared for ridicule, because some girls are bound to think *we* think we're better. They'll call us "holier than thou." But God knows we're just trying to answer his call. He knows, and now we're reminded how much is riding on it.

Food for Thought

You've heard this before, but never enough: "No one can serve two masters" (Matthew 6:24). You're either for Jesus or for the world.

Second Thoughts

Loving God and your neighbor are two good ways to imitate Jesus.

Divine Thoughts

Dearest Jesus, it's really hard to be in the world, yet separated from it. But with your help, I can do it. Amen.

Your Thoughts:

Section 10

Perfect Peace

Devotion 87

"Get rid of all bitterness, rage, anger, harsh words, and slander, as well as all types of evil behavior."

Ephesians 4:31 NLT

Keeping the Peace

Dara won first prize in the community art contest, and she was on cloud nine. But not everyone shared her joy. In fact, Else, the class bully, took this as her dump-on-Dara opportunity.

"Hey, Dara," Else yelled. "What did you do, throw up on the canvas? That's what your painting looks like: Dork vomit."

Dara ached to lob a comeback in Else's face. But she swallowed her anger, then did the smart thing. She flagged down her BFF, and the two girls walked off.

When a bully gets her claws in us, our first thoughts are probably something like, *Boy, would I like to super glue her mouth shut.* That's only natural. Bullies tend to bring out the worst in us—not the best. So, what do we do? Okay, we didn't start the trouble, and it isn't fair, for sure. But we can restore our composure and take back at least *some* control by the way we respond outside and inside.

Experts have a lot of opinions about how to outwardly deal with bullies. We have oodles of info on our Faithgirlz website about handling specific situations, and Faithgirlz bullying expert, Nancy Rue, has awesome step-by-step solutions in her book, *Girl Politics* (pages 87-132).

A practical coping mechanism that can always be useful, though, is to try to stop bullies from derailing what's inside—our peace of mind and well-being in Christ. For that, we have to pray hard for the Holy Spirit's help to avoid dwelling on the situation and ask him to flood our minds with Whatever (something lovely, excellent, or praiseworthy, for example).

See, we've already been hurt once by the bully's actions. But with the Helper's grace, we don't have to *continue* to feel badly. We don't have to let what happened ruin our day/week. We don't have to waste time rehashing stuff or plotting how to get even. We don't have to "sin by letting anger control" us (Ephesians 4:26 NLT).

Easy to say, we know. But that's what Jesus did. When the bully Pharisees said he was the devil because he cast out demons, Jesus replied calmly, "How can Satan cast out Satan?"(Mark 3:23 NLT). And that was the end of it.

Jesus let it go. And that's what we need to do: refuse to let a bully's actions hold our thoughts prisoner. Instead, let's pray for strength to clear our minds and then forget about it.

Food for Thought

If you're being threatened physically, or if bullying is affecting school or sports, or making you depressed, run, don't walk, to get help from an adult.

Second Thoughts

Bullying is the pits. But it can give you an opportunity to act like Jesus by forgiving and keeping inner peace when things are difficult.

Divine Thoughts

Sweet Jesus, I want to be like you and love my enemies. But it's, like, way hard. Please help me. Amen.

Your Thoughts:

Devotion 88

"Blessed are the peacemakers, for they will be called children of God."

Matthew 5:9 NRSV

Peacemaking 101

Jackie and Maureen were friends until a stupid fight over computer time in the lab left them angry and spiteful towards each other. Connie, who was friends with both girls, felt if she could just get them to talk, there was a good chance they could patch things up.

If she failed, though, she knew she'd lose *both* friends. Still, Connie felt God calling her to do something. So she prayed for the Holy Spirit's help, then asked the girls to her house for a pizza pow-wow. And God rewarded her efforts: Maureen and Jackie finally agreed to get past their anger, forgive each other, and work things out—including a fixed schedule for time on the computer.

We all can't be at ease being "peacemakers." But some girls just have a knack for it. God has blessed them with leadership capabilities that include a humble, logical, patient personality. And since other girls tend to respect and look up to them, the Helper can use their abilities as a "go-between" for God's glory. The Bible says if God gives us a gift "to encourage others," we should do so (Romans 12:6–8 NLT).

The apostle Barnabas (whose nickname was "Encourager") had this skill. The Bible says he was "full of the Holy Spirit and faith" (Acts 11:24), and went regularly to the early churches to help people stop arguing and start getting along.

Okay, but peacemaking isn't just limited to sitting down with girls trying to resolve stuff. We're all called to "aim for harmony in the church and try to build each other up" (Romans 14:19 NLT). That means we keep an open mind, never say or write anything that will pit girls against each other, and treat everyone the way we want to be treated. Here are some other ways we can be peacemakers:

- ♥ Refuse to take part in gossip; don't jump to conclusions.
- ♥ Listen to and show respect for other's opinions.
- ♥ Avoid a confrontation by taking a "You first" attitude.
- ♥ Think Whatever thoughts.
- ♥ Turn the other cheek; be humble.
- ♥ Let things go; don't take offense so easily.
- ♥ Avoid rivalries.
- ♥ Don't be a busybody or a tattletale.

For sure, there's, like, way too much arguing, nastiness, and violence in the world. The Bible says with God's help, "peacemakers will plant seeds of peace and reap a harvest of righteousness" (James 3:18 NLT). So let's get busy planting, so we can begin to start reaping.

Food for Thought

There *is* a limit as to how far you can go to keep things calm. You can't pretend something is right that's wrong just to keep the peace.

Second Thoughts

Jesus was beaten so that we might have peace (Isaiah 53:5). Remember this and praise him often.

Divine Thoughts

Dearest Jesus, help me be a peacemaker, not a peace breaker, wherever I am. Amen.

Your Thoughts:

Devotion 89

"You will keep in perfect peace,
all who trust in you,
all whose thoughts are fixed on you."
Isaiah 26:3 NLT

A Piece of Your Day

Julie's calendar was getting out of hand. Between school, homework, violin, babysitting, sleepovers, soccer, dentist appointments, doing her chores, her science project, track, community service, texting her friends, and keeping up with her blog and twittering—she began to feel like the white rabbit in *Alice in Wonderland*. She was always checking the time and always coming up short.

Truth is she was overwhelmed with commitments and activities. Being constantly "on" began to leave her feeling stressed and hyper. So much so that when she *did* have some down-time, her mind was still racing. She was so wound up, she found it impossible to relax. For sure, her thoughts weren't fixed on the Lord (Isaiah 26:3). Maybe a quick grace at meals, and a prayer before bed. So it's no wonder she couldn't find any peace.

Sound familiar? Okay, so maybe we're not as bad as Julie. But we all do seem to have a gi-normous amount on our plates. And that's not altogether a bad thing. Obviously, God doesn't want us to sit on the sidelines. The Bible says Jesus came so we could enjoy life "to the full" (John 10:10). Still, that doesn't mean he wants our days to be so filled we freak out. And he certainly doesn't want us to have such a hectic schedule, there's no room for him.

When we find ourselves in a situation like this, we need to push the stop button, make a list of our commitments, and prioritize. We need to list the absolutely-positively-must-do items, weed out the non-essentials, and come up with a more realistic, peaceful plan for our days—one that includes specific time for prayer and time to think about and thank our Lord for his sacrifice and his goodness.

People don't like to feel they're being "squeezed into" a friend's schedule. And that's the way Jesus is apt to feel if we cram more and more into our agendas, leaving hardly any time for him.

Jesus should top our priority list, and if that means we have to spend less time on social media, or substitute Bible class for debate club, well, then, that's what needs to be done. After all, if we want Jesus to keep us in perfect peace, he won't be interested in how much we include in our day, but how much of our day includes him.

Food for Thought

Talk about grueling schedules! Jesus was always in demand to heal and teach. Yet he always made time for prayers (Mark 1:35).

Second Thoughts

Here's a short prayer you can say throughout the day from Isaiah 26:12 NLT: "Lord, you grant us peace; all we have accomplished is really from you."

Divine Thoughts

Dearest Jesus, sometimes I'm so rushed, I don't make time for you. But that's going to stop. Amen.

Your Thoughts:

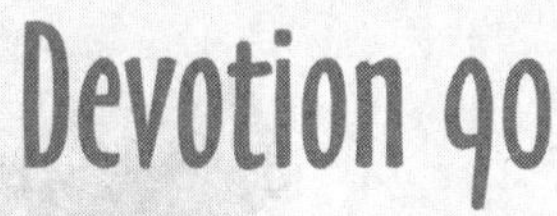

Devotion 90

"Whatever you have learned or received or heard from me, or seen in me—put it into practice. And the God of peace will be with you."

Philippians 4:9

Whatever . . . Keeps You Peaceful

"Yikes," Janice said to her friend Amiee. "I'm, like, totally freaked about this hurricane. What if a tree falls on our house? What if my stuff gets ruined? And Ginny's sleepover is next week. What if ..."

The devil is always trying to mess up our thoughts and steal our peace—whether it's sending our imaginations on a wild-goose chase with frightening what ifs, making us feel we're inadequate or inferior, or creeping us out with uneasiness and dread.

Reason enough why the apostle Paul told us to keep our thoughts on the Whatever values and on Jesus—who offers us a peace of mind strong enough to conquer Satan's pull and give us a quiet heart in the midst of life's storms.

Now Jesus said "Peace I leave with you; *My peace* I give

you" (John 14:27, emphasis added). And we can be sure if Jesus is offering us peace, it's not like any other we've ever known.

In fact, he told us as much: "And the peace I give is a gift the world cannot give," he said. "So don't be troubled or afraid" (John 14:27 NLT). The feeling of well-being the world offers is temporary and depends on things like doing well in school, or money, or feeling accepted/popular. But that sense of contentment can be gone in a flash if we lose those things.

The peace Jesus offers isn't tied to stuff. It's tied to him. So it's powerful and permanent. Paul described the feeling as "so great we cannot understand it" (Philippians 4:7 NCV). Plus, it's infinitely more precious because Jesus paid for it with his life. "Therefore," Paul explained, "since we have been made right in God's sight by faith, we have peace with God because of what Jesus Christ our Lord has done for us" (Romans 5:1 NLT).

Filling our heads with these kinds of thoughts will keep our minds at ease no matter what. It's the sense of calm Paul kept even when he was ridiculed, beaten, jailed, and stoned. And it's why he urged us not to "worry about anything, instead pray about everything" (Philippians 4:6 TLB). Because if we practice what Paul preached, we can be less stressed knowing that "the God of peace" is and will be with us always (Philippians 4:9).

Can't think of anything better; can you?

Food for Thought

Feeling stressed? Concentrate on Jesus, his Word, and the Whatever values, and nothing can rattle you ... unless you let it.

Second Thoughts

The bumper sticker wisdom of "No God? No peace; Know God? Know peace" says it all in eight words.

Divine Thoughts

Dear Jesus, thank you for making peace with your Father for me. Amen.

Your Thoughts: